PIRATE HUNTER
THE LIFE OF CAPTAIN
WOODES ROGERS

PIRATE HUNTER
THE LIFE OF CAPTAIN
WOODES ROGERS

Graham A. Thomas

Pen & Sword
MARITIME

First published in Great Britain in 2008 and reprinted in 2009 by
PEN & SWORD MARITIME
an imprint of
Pen & Sword Books Ltd
47 Church Street
Barnsley
South Yorkshire
S70 2AS

Copyright © Graham A. Thomas, 2008

ISBN 978 1 84415 808 9

The right of Graham A. Thomas to be identified as author of
this work has been asserted by him in accordance with
the Copyright, Designs and Patents Act 1988.

A CIP catalogue record for this book is
available from the British Library.

Several illustrations in the plate section were originally published in James Poling's
book, *The Man Who Saved Robinson Crusoe*. Attempts have been made to contact
the copyright holder without success. If anyone has any knowledge or information
pertaining to the copyright please contact the publisher.

Printed and bound in Great Britain
by CPI UK

Pen & Sword Books Ltd incorporates the imprints of
Pen & Sword Aviation, Pen & Sword Maritime, Pen & Sword Military,
Wharncliffe Local History, Pen & Sword Select, Pen & Sword Military Classics,
Leo Cooper, Remember When, Seaforth Publishing and Frontline Publishing.

For a complete list of Pen & Sword titles please contact
PEN & SWORD BOOKS LIMITED
47 Church Street, Barnsley, South Yorkshire, S70 2AS, England
E-mail: enquiries@pen-and-sword.co.uk
Website: www.pen-and-sword.co.uk

Contents

To all the heroes big and small, young and old throughout the world; and to Julie, a true heroine.

List of Illustrations

The street where Rogers's house stood in Queen Square Bristol as it is today.

This photograph, taken from the centre of the square, shows the building bearing a plaque that commemorates Rogers and his house which stood in this spot.

A view of the Bristol dockyards today. Even now there are masts to be seen in a replica galleon tied up near the SS *Great Britain*.

Another view of the docks today: Rogers's house in Queen Square was only a short walk to the docks. Though today the masts of large sailing vessels are gone we can imagine what it must have been like.

The *Duke* sets sail: an illustration of the *Duke* leaving the docks in Bristol for the round the world voyage.

The *Duke* rounds the Horn: the *Duke* and *Dutchess* round Cape Horn in appalling weather in order to get into Pacific waters to plunder the Spanish vessels sailing from Manila to Acapulco.

Selkirk comes aboard: Lord Selkirk was found by Rogers stranded on Juan Fernández Island and his rescue and subsequent story formed the basis for the famous yarn *Robinson Crusoe* by Daniel Defoe.

Careening the *Duke*: throughout the voyage, Rogers regularly careened both the *Duke* and the *Dutchess* in order to get as much speed as possible from both the little frigates.

Attacking the galleon: this illustration shows the *Duke* in action against the first Manila ship which proved to be loaded with treasure.

Battle on the deck: snipers fire on a Spanish vessel as the *Duke* closes in for the capture.

Rogers is wounded: during the action against the Manila ship Rogers was wounded, a shot hitting him in the jaw. But while lying on the deck bleeding he continued to give orders by writing them out.

Taking the Manila ship: this illustration shows the unsuccessful attempt by Rogers to take the second, much larger Manila ship.

Aerial view of Fort Charlotte: this fort overlooking Nassau was rebuilt several years after Rogers's second stint as governor of the Bahamas.

Another view of Fort Charlotte on New Providence Island near Nassau.

Another view of Fort Charlotte, showing how it must have looked when Rogers was governor.

Government House: Rogers had Government House built while he was governor of the Bahamas and this is how it looks today.

A computer drawing showing what is left of the ruins of the old fort at Nassau.

This hut, though built for tourists, is a good example of what the huts on the island must have looked like when Rogers first arrived at Nassau as governor.

Preface

When I first discovered Woodes Rogers while researching another book I became fascinated by the man. His life spanned little more than fifty years, yet during that time he sailed around the world, fought on land and at sea, captured a treasure ship, was made Governor of the Bahamas and was responsible for ridding that little settlement of Nassau on New Providence of some of the worst pirates and cutthroats around.

We all know about Blackbeard and Captain Kidd; but we do not necessarily know about Woodes Rogers. When I set out to write this book I thought it would be about his time as Governor of New Providence in the Bahamas and his hunting down the pirates. But I soon became aware of the general principle that you cannot look at one particular time of a person's life without taking in the whole; in Woodes Rogers's case it was the totality of his experiences that made him what he was when he first arrived in the Bahamas. As Governor he orchestrated the hunt for and capture of the pirates, organized their trial, passed sentence and ensured they were hanged. The tales of the pirates Josiah Bunce and Jack Rackham that I have included here seem almost unbelievable, but the same details and facts appear in several different sources, such as, for example, Daniel Defoe's *The Pyrates*, *The Funnel of Gold* by Mendel Peterson and *Under the Black Flag* by David Cordingly. The last two authors take great pains to ensure that they treat the actions of these pirates as fact rather than sensation. One can only assume, then, that the facts taken down during the trial of the pirates who had aided and abetted Josiah Bunce were already sensationalized; what was being said was believed by everyone at the court to have been the truth. It is quite likely that word of mouth about the actions of these pirates travelled fast and was embellished as it went from person to person. The truth could then have been mixed in with sensation.

In addition to the secondary sources mentioned above (and detailed in the further reading section at the end of this book), my research is based on primary documents, found in the Bristol City Archives, the British Library, the National Maritime Museum and, above all, in the National Archives at Kew. These latter include the actual notes from the trial of the pirates themselves, and many other documents from the Colonial Office papers (Americas and West Indies volumes for the years 1726–32), such as abstracts of the council meetings at Nassau and letters from Woodes Rogers to the Secretary of State and others. Woodes Rogers's own journal, later published as *A Cruising Voyage Round the World*, is of course another major source of information.

I have tried to ascertain the facts because I am interested in Woodes Rogers and what he did. We know from his many letters that he feared an imminent attack by Charles Vane, Blackbeard and many other pirates, but that his main worry was not the pirates but the Spanish in Cuba, only a stone's throw away from the Bahamas. While fighting the Spanish on his voyage round the world he was wounded twice yet continued to order his men and keep the battle going while in excruciating pain, showing courage and determination.

The various sources I have used to write this book rarely mention the man himself, though we can glean things from his letters and his actions. For example, he was a prolific reader interested in the voyages of other sailors and adventurers: Bryan Little states in his *Crusoe's Captain* that in his cabin on the *Duke* Rogers had books about round-the-world voyages by Italian and French seafarers, for example Dampier's,[1] as well as books on climate and weather – anything for inspiration to mount his audacious plans.

At the very core of the man was an experienced seafarer who loved nothing more than to stand on the deck of his ship and feel the wind in his face and the spray of the sea coming over the bows. But he was also a man with an eye to the main chance, the chance for adventure and profit and to further expand British influence around the world.

It is clear that Rogers was a dreamer, a man with ideas that preoccupied him. He planned trips to Madagascar, to set up an English settlement there, and spent many hours poring over whatever books there were on the island. He followed his father on voyages from Bristol to the Newfoundland's Grand Banks. But I would like to go further and speculate that Rogers was obsessed by setting English settlements in far-flung places. I say this because he was always working on ideas and put them into practice whenever he could.

On his world voyage he was a privateer backed by influential British merchants with tacit approval from the government. His mission was to sail into Pacific waters and take whatever Spanish treasure he could. So to all intents and purposes he was a pirate, too, though he felt himself above them because he was sanctioned by a British government that was at war with Spain. A patriot, he was deeply loyal to the Crown. He was a family man, too: but his marriage broke down. When he went to the Bahamas he left his wife behind in England, and when he returned he was a different man. The marriage could not continue.

When he became Governor he was on the other side of the fence, facing the pirates down and dealing with them. He made those islands safe for the colony there to flourish and brought back stability; but lack of resources, lack of money almost wrecked his work. Undaunted, he pushed on until poor health forced him to return to Bristol.

Rogers was a hero. He was a tough commander, a kind and fair man. But always, the threat from the Spanish and from pirates was just over the horizon.

A remarkable man: this is his story.

Graham A. Thomas
January 2008

Introduction

When Will The Pirates Come?

By encouraging the loose people here, even some of my own soldiers, palatines and French that came before me they had privately consulted to leave the settlement. Nay some of the ringleaders had secretly agreed to seize and destroy me and my officers and deliver up the fort for the use of the pirates. I having timely notice of it found three of the principals and punished them with a severe whipping but having no power for holding a court martial and cannot spare the men to send them hence I shall release them and be the more on my guard.[2]

(Woodes Rogers, Governor of New Providence, 24 January 1718)

Over the horizon lay a terror that could destroy the little settlement of New Providence. The hot tropical breeze tugged at Woodes Rogers's coat as he paced the battlements of the crumbling fort that overlooked the harbour. Everywhere around him the fort was in ruins, strewn with debris and rotting vegetation that he knew he must clear and repair if they were to survive.

As the first Governor of New Providence, Rogers worried about the dangers for his men and the few inhabitants: not only did they face disease, but also pirates. Since his arrival, Rogers had managed to push the pirates out of the settlement, away from the island, and brought relative peace and security to its inhabitants. But he knew the threat was not far away. He had sent letter after letter to England asking for assistance, more money, more resources, a Royal Navy presence; but there had been only silence. He stared out over the harbour, the hot sun beating down on him as he watched his men toil with repairs to the fort. He could not understand why England remained silent.

His aim was to rebuild the defences, secure the fort, place guns to protect the harbour and wait. Most of the men who had arrived with him were ill with fever and the few indigenous natives were of little help. He knew that at any sunrise he could look over the horizon and see Spanish ships heading straight for the island or, worse, pirates. He wondered how long the reformed pirates of the settlement would stay reformed, and how many might rise up against him.

The word pirates conjures up popular images of Captain Hook and his men, loveable rogues we know won't really hurt Peter Pan. But fact is very different from legend. Pirates were murderers and thieves, plundering, raping and pillaging. Their lives were dangerous, hard and short. Few pirates lived into old age or died peacefully in their beds. Many were hung by the state, killed in battle or killed by their own crew. At the beginning of the eighteenth century pirates flourished in the West Indies and the Americas, with names such as Captain Edward Teach, Captain Charles Vane, Captain Jack Rackham – the stuff of legends.

There were also those determined to stop the pirates' reign of terror and restore order. Woodes Rogers was one of these, though before he came to the island as its first Governor he was no better than a pirate himself, plundering Spanish ships and settlements on a round the world voyage as a British privateer sanctioned by the English government, since England and Spain were locked in a struggle for supremacy of the seas.

Rogers, the son of a sea captain, was born in Bristol in 1679. The family had originally come from Poole, but on their arrival in Bristol they set about making connections with the important people of the city and by the time he was a boy the family had gained a prominent place in the Bristol social scene. Rogers took firm advantage of their position and by 1705 had married Sarah, the daughter of Admiral Sir William Whetstone. In the same year Rogers was made a freeman of Bristol. Just three years later, in 1708, and already an experienced seaman himself, he organized and commanded a voyage that would see him circumnavigate the globe. The mayor and the Corporation of Bristol sponsored the voyage and a royal commission from the Lord High Admiral gave Rogers the permission he needed to attack and plunder enemy vessels.

Securing the services of William Dampier, a 56-year-old navigator who had already navigated the globe twice, Rogers prepared to leave. His expedition consisted of two ships, the *Duke* of 310 tons and thirty guns and the 260-ton *Dutchess*. On 2 August 1708 the expedition weighed anchor and set sail on the epic journey, heading south for the Canary Islands. Throughout this voyage Rogers put down several mutinies, survived storms, attacked the Spanish wherever he could and captured several vessels. In one battle, off the coast of California, he was badly wounded when a bullet struck him in the left cheek. Most people would have been rolling on the deck in agony, but not Rogers. Indeed, only a few days later he was wounded again while on deck during a ferocious engagement with a 60-ton Spanish ship. As cannon shot smashed into the ships a wood splinter cut through his ankle. Despite his wounds he continued giving orders, directing the attack and keeping his men under control.

In 1711 Rogers returned to England with an impressive booty of gold bullion, precious stones and silks plundered from the vessels he had captured. Two-thirds of the spoils went to the sponsors and owners of the expedition; the rest was divided up among the officers and the crew.

A year later the journal of his voyage around the world was published to great acclaim. Indeed, it was the basis for Daniel Defoe's classic novel *Robinson Crusoe*.

The Bahamas had become the headquarters of pirates in the West Indies, and with no Royal Navy ships in the area they were free to roam, plunder and murder at will, threatening to bring trading to a halt. Something had to be done to drive the pirates out, restore order and free the trade routes.

A capable, tough and energetic man was needed to suppress such piracy. That man was Woodes Rogers. Because of the success of his voyage around the world and in successfully attacking enemy ships, London and Bristol merchants could find no other man so suitable for the job. He was given a brief to put down piracy by whatever means and carried with him a royal pardon from the king to be granted to any pirate who surrendered to him before 15 September 1718.

I am sorry to see His Majesty's goodness has no more effect of those villains that are still out, and doubt unless His Majesty's own ships in these parts exert themselves more and are stationed under the directions for the Governor in proper places to destroy the pirates, it will be very hard to resist the remainder and if it is not soon done I fear they will again grow more numerous.

I have now an account of one Captain Longor. That commands two pirate ships of thirty-six guns each, who designs to come hither to offer to surrender themselves and to embrace His Majesty's gracious pardon, and the time being so far elapsed, I would if I could resist them, but the inhabitants here are so frightened that I fear I shall be forced to receive them at all hazards, if I do, I will send an expedition immediately for England, and in the mean time manage them as well as I can.

Should the Spaniards attack us and if they do with the small numbers I now have I shall be in a mean condition to hold out and should the pirates come first, it may be best to receive them to defend myself against the Spaniards, for if I refuse to receive them, most of those I have now with me will either join them or quit me, and then they'll posses the place with nothing I can propose to do against them. (Woodes Rogers, Governor of New Providence, 30 January 1719)

On 11 April 1718 Rogers set sail aboard the East Indiaman *Delicia* in company with HMS *Milford* and HMS *Rose* and two sloops. Having sent HMS *Rose* ahead of the squadron, they arrived in Nassau to find a French ship burning, set alight by pirate Captain Charles Vane in an effort to stop the British. But with the arrival of the rest of the squadron Vane fled and Rogers took possession of the fort at New Providence.

The fort was in a terrible state and had to be repaired if it was to be capable of defending the town at all. Rogers mounted cannon on the battlements to protect the harbour and sent out Captain Hornigold, a former pirate who had accepted the king's pardon, to capture Vane. While the men he had landed with toiled under the heat and humidity rebuilding the fort Rogers set up a council, appointed a secretary general and a chief justice.

Shortly after landing several of the men succumbed to illness and disease, severely limiting Rogers's resources. Though the situation was precarious Rogers felt that, if he could get the fort ready, he could make a stand against attack by pirates or the Spanish.

I don't doubt but we should have had abundance more inhabitants of the substance settled here, those at Anguilla and the Virgin Islands that are of no value to the crown, I hear are coming to settle here, from Carolina, Bermuda and other ports will also come as soon as they heard that we can make a stand against the Spaniards. (Woodes Rogers, Governor of the Bahamas, 24 January 1719)

While the men worked feverishly repairing the fort, Hornigold was pursuing Vane, but after several days Vane eluded him. Instead, Hornigold captured ten pirates on the island of Exuma. Determined to make an example of these men, on 9 December 1718 Rogers convened an Admiralty Court in His Majesty's guardroom in Nassau. The court found the ten men guilty of betraying the king's pardon and returning to piracy and had them executed at the fort, signalling the end of the pirates' hold over the Bahamas.

Law and order may have come to the islands, but the threat of piracy and the

Spanish lay just over the horizon, as Rogers knew. So he continued the work of rebuilding their defences. To prevent surprise attacks he set up three companies of militia. Gun carriages were made for unmounted cannon, and a palisade was built around the fort. The streets had become overgrown by the jungle vegetation, so Rogers had them cleared. But with only a tiny force, many sick from fever, progress was slow. In addition to this, the lack of resources and constant threat of attack from pirates and the Spanish, there was no answer to his pleas for help from England. Feeling increasingly cut off he pressed on with his plans. In 1720 he wrote to the Board of Trade and Plantations declaring that the Royal Navy had abandoned him and left him with a few sick men to combat hundreds of pirates. Still there was only silence from London. Finally, having had enough, his health failing, Rogers returned to England.

Many books have been written about pirates and their murderous ways. Few have been written about the men who tried to stop them. Under intense difficulty, Woodes Rogers managed to bring security and stability to the Bahamas. Using his own letters and his journal, this book tells the story of Woodes Rogers, privateer, Governor and pirate hunter.

Chapter 1

The Rogers Family

Rogers had two spells as Governor of the Bahamas and died in office. But he left a lasting legacy in that tiny colony that became the seed from which the Bahamas as we know them today sprang.

In the early months of 1729 Rogers was in London preparing for his second term as Governor. It was during this visit that the famous and only painting of him as the main subject was painted by Hogarth.

But his second term in office was to be fraught with intrigue and spite that would ruin his health and lead to his death. He had two major enemies at the end of his life. His worst enemy had always been his health, which gradually deteriorated. About that he could do little but, as we will see later, about his other enemies, those men who would challenge his authority, he could do a great deal.

Before we look at the part of his life which brought him face to face with the pirates during his first governorship, we need to look at the period before he became governor, when he was a privateer and sailed round the world, when he saved Lord Selkirk and when his exploits became the inspiration for Daniel Defoe's *Robinson Crusoe*.

It is necessary now to go back to the beginning to see how his experiences made him the man he was, capable of dealing with pirates and ultimately bringing order to a lawless settlement. Rogers was a product of his age, his family and his position in life. His family belonged to the country gentry, and no doubt some of his illustrious ancestors played a part in building his character. The recorded history of the Rogers family goes as far back as the fifteenth century, when documents show the family was settled in East Dorset near Blandford. Through marriages they formed alliances with some of the best families in the county – Stourton, Luttrell, Courtenay and Seymour can be seen in the Rogers's genealogy. Indeed, the coats of arms of these families were with the Rogers's arms in the family chapel in the old church at Blandford.

Sir John Rogers was one of the more illustrious of the family. He sat in

Parliament as the Knight of the Shire and was also Sheriff of Dorset; when he died in 1565 an alabaster tomb was built in the family chapel that showed his sixteen sons and four daughters around him along the sides of the tomb. At the time of his death, only nine sons were alive. In the mid-sixteenth century the family moved down to Poole to take advantage of the town's bustling commerce, trade and navigation. But, while continuing to live and thrive in Poole, the family also continued to form alliances and make connections with some of the more prosperous Salisbury families. In 1572 a John Rogers was mayor of Poole, while, in a will from a local merchant, William Webbe, who died in 1554, he made mention of land purchased from Sir John Rogers and given to his son-in-law Robert Rogers. This Robert is one of the seven sons who died before his father.

The port of Poole then flourished as a Channel port, but when the navigation routes to commerce in the Atlantic opened up, Poole came into its own. Near the end of the century, around 1583, merchant ships from the town were navigating across the ocean to the Newfoundland fisheries, taking the cod and bringing it back for consumption in Britain. The busy port continued to expand as more trade routes opened up over the centuries along what is now the American coast down to the Carolinas.

In this environment the Rogers family became involved in a variety of different trades. One Robert Rogers (not the one named above) was a leather-seller in London, but in Poole founded a series of almshouses for old couples. There was a blacksmith named John Rogers who married into the Woods family. His wife was named Ann and his son was christened Woods, though not the subject of this book. This Woods Rogers had a son who was also called Woodes and was christened in 1650.

By the mid-seventeenth century the Rogers family had become Puritan in their religious convictions, in keeping with the temperament of the town of Poole. During the English Civil War, Poole backed Parliament and was a small supporter of parliamentary power in an area that otherwise supported the king. According to Bryan Little, well after the Civil War and after Charles II came to power, Poole remained Puritan, often being referred to as a hotbed of sedition, Dissenters, Whigs, Exclusionists and Monmouth partisans. By 1683 Woodes Rogers was probably a little boy playing in Poole harbour, crowded with the masts of ships regularly plying the sea routes between England and Newfoundland.

Captain Woodes Rogers was the third man in the Rogers lineage to carry that name and, unlike his father, the second Woodes Rogers, mystery surrounds his birth, education and early life. The second Woodes Rogers was a Freeman of the Borough and in the listing of the poll tax of 1690 his calling was that of mariner. As master of the *Endeavour* he entered Poole in 1683 carrying a cargo of olive oil, brandy, rice, Castille soap and wine after a run from Alicante in Spain. This Woodes Rogers also set sail for Newfoundland carrying a cargo of salt for curing cod later that same year. This man of the sea was not in the list of merchants exporting from Poole that was published two years later.

In 1690 his daughter Mary was baptized at St James at Poole and a son, John, was christened there two years earlier. But this son was not the eldest. In the tradition of naming the oldest son after the father, the eldest was Woodes Rogers, the third of the Rogers family to carry this name and our hero.

In early 1705 Rogers was married and was said to have been about 25 years old; but there is no record of where he was born. If he was a native of Poole no church registers or records mention his baptism, so we can only assume he was born around 1678 or 1679. At the time of his birth, the parson of St James in Poole was one Samuel Hardy, a strong Puritan whose beliefs put him in good stead with the Puritan congregation in Poole, though he was regarded as a Nonconformist and corrupter of people by the Dorset Royalists and Tories. Indeed, Anthony Ettrick, the Poole Recorder of the day, suggested that Hardy administered the scriptures, baptized and took burials without using the Book of Common Prayer. Having strayed away from the Church of England, Hardy was to be later removed; but during his time at St James there were very few entries in the registry of marriages, births and deaths for a town the size of Poole. 'Parish after parish is known to be incomplete for the actual Commonwealth years,' Bryan Little wrote in his splendid book *Crusoe's Captain*.

As far as his education is concerned there is virtually nothing that indicates what schools Rogers went to or how much schooling he had. From the journal of his voyage round the world and from letters written to the Admiralty during his time as Governor of the Bahamas it was evident that his spelling and choice of phrasing did not reflect those of a scholar. We can only assume that he attended the local grammar school and that his knowledge of navigation and seafaring came from accompanying his father on trips in the Channel or on voyages to Newfoundland.

Records do show that at almost the end of the century the Rogers family moved from their home in Poole to Bristol. In the Bristol City Archives Rogers is described as 'the son of Woodes Rogers mariner' resident in the city of Bristol, who was apprenticed to John and Thomasina Yeamans.

The Yeamans were a family of good standing amongst the Bristol merchants, traders and seaman, so an apprenticeship to such a family would have great consequences and lead to a strong and influential position in society. However, another major inducement for procuring an apprenticeship was that at the end of the seven-year period the apprentice would be a freeman with voting rights or citizenship of the city. This privilege was vital for any newcomer in making a fortune for himself and becoming part of the tight community of Bristol merchants.

So in 1697 the third Woodes Rogers began his apprenticeship at the age of 18 in Bristol, which indicates that around this time the Rogers family moved to that city. However, records show that in 1693 there was a Bristol merchant, Francis Rogers, a joint owner of the *Delavall*, a privateer sent out that year against the French. Whether or not this Rogers was a relative cannot be confirmed; however, he was one of the main owners of the two privateers that Woodes Rogers took out on his voyage round the world in 1708, so it is possible that the Rogers family already had connections in Bristol before Woodes Rogers took up his apprenticeship.

Rogers received his freedom of the city not through serving his long apprenticeship but by marrying the daughter of a freeman, which was an equally valid way of gaining influence. Through their connections in Bristol society the Rogers family were to make the acquaintance of the naval officer Captain William Whetstone. Rogers was to marry Sarah, Whetstone's only daughter and heir.

In 1696 and 1697 Whetstone commanded the fourth-rate *Dreadnought*, escorting the fishing fleets from Poole to the Newfoundland Grand Banks fishing grounds for protection from French attacks on the fleets and the fishery settlers there. For a family originally from Poole Whetstone's exploits in supporting the fishing grounds and trade routes between the colony and Poole would have brought great sympathy.

England had two major enemies at this time, France and Spain. Rogers's exploits were directed against Spain. This was the time of the Spanish Succession. The Infante Don Baltasar Carlos, son to King Philip IV of Spain, though a healthy little boy died of illness in his teens. The crown then fell to Charles II, reigning at the same time as England's Charles II. This Spanish

Charles was the son of Philip IV by his second wife and suffered throughout his life from a deformity. He was known as Charles the 'Bewitched' and in 1700 died a childless king despite his two marriages. He failed to continue the line and continue the Habsburg dynasty.

The conflict that resulted was the War of the the Spanish Succession, fought for the disposition of the Spanish crown and the vast Spanish possessions, a war in which Woodes Rogers made his fortune. King Philip V of Spain, placed on the Spanish throne by the French, was England's enemy.

By the opening of the war Whetstone was acting Rear Admiral and commanding, in the West Indies, a small squadron reinforcing Admiral Benbow, who was mortally wounded in the battle against French Admiral du Casse. In 1702 Whetstone took over from Benbow after his death, at a time when his only son was killed while in action with a French privateer; two years later Whetstone was commanding a squadron in the Channel.

The Rogers family had already moved from Poole to Bristol. In 1700 Rogers senior was commanding a small Bristol ship, the *Elizabeth* on the routes to Newfoundland. The city records show that in 1702 a lease was granted to Woodes Rogers (Sr) 'of this city, mariner'. Located on the south side of Queen Square the dimensions for this plot were 42 feet wide by 108 feet deep. A substantial house was to be built on this plot, spanning its full breadth. Built of brick and stone dressings and with a brick enclosed front courtyard, the building was completed in 1704. The square was named in honour of England's new sovereign, Queen Anne, and was the latest fashionable area of the city. This quarter was the beginning of the process that would give Bristol a series of residential squares and terraces of space and refinement.

The Whetstones also moved into this area, where the houses there would have looked over the muddy Avon. However, Woodes Rogers's father died at sea between 1705 and 1706 and had little chance to see the new house. By this time, Rogers, the subject of this book, was a married man: his marriage to Sarah Whetstone in the City of London church St Mary Magdalene in Fish Street had taken place in January 1705. Now the son-in-law of a Bristol Freeman, Admiral Whetstone, Rogers was admitted to the liberties of the City of Bristol, and his marriage reinforced his local standing.

Whetstone himself was sent to the Caribbean and returned within two years. No doubt several conversations between Rogers and Whetstone would have inspired and informed the young man. It is even likely that Whetstone provided Rogers with contacts in parts of Spain's vast holdings in the Americas.

Chapter 2

The Spanish Empire

King Philip IV of Spain had a son, Baltasar Carlos, who, though a healthy little boy, became ill during his teens and died. When Philip died the succession fell on his other son, by his second marriage. This was 'Charles the Bewitched', a deformed individual who in turn died in 1700, without issue to continue the dynasty, sparking off the War of the Spanish Succession. This war would have an influence throughout the Spanish American and West Indian colonies. Central America, Mexico, South and South-Western America and most of South America, except Brazil, were allied to whichever king would end up sitting on the throne in Madrid. Spanish rule also extended to Puerto Rico, Cuba and eastern Santo Domingo to Pensacola and St Augustine in Florida.

In 1709 and 1710 the coastline extending from Chile to the present border between Mexico and the United States had plenty of areas where attacks on the Spanish could be mounted, landings made and escapes executed before any sort of real counter-attack could be set up. The strongest towns and ports like Cartagena, Panama, or Portobello had excellent defences, but the vast areas in between like the empty coasts and lightly defended towns were ripe targets for the privateer and pirate.

Even so, the Spanish had had two centuries to build up life in Latin America, to impose European Spain on their colonies, to the point where Spain's human resources were drained so that her way of life and ideals could be imposed on her colonies. The death of 'Charles the Bewitched' without issue in the very early years of the eighteenth century threw shadows over the life and rule of the colonial regime despite its being so well established; now the contest to decide who would rule Spain began.

Bastions of Spanish rule, the towns, though spread out, were strategically important to the Spanish for trade and government. Panama, for example, had been rebuilt on a new site, heavily fortified with a new cathedral. Throughout her American colonies Spain imposed the same municipal pattern of European life as thoroughly as possible, by designing the cities and towns in the Spanish part of the Indies and South America as mirror images of those from the mother country that would rival any European city at that time. While the English colonies of America were far less elaborate the Spanish American colonies were well planned and developed: behind the walled gates the streets would be laid out in the grids, squares and rectangles that now are the basis for towns and cities across the United States and Canada.

Yet for all of the sophistication of the Spanish colonies there were great tracts of land that had yet to be explored or even partially subdued. Bryan Little states that foreign visitors to Mexico found that many of the native Indians hated their Spanish rulers and would rise up against them if the right opportunity presented itself. Even along the coast of Peru Spanish rule was nominal, with a priest and church constituting the only elements of a Spanish way of life.

But in the towns in South America controlled by Spain, economic life flourished under a doctrine that dictated that the overseas trade from Spanish America was there to support Spain itself, and any of Spain's campaigns closer to home were to be wholly financed with trade from the Indies. The Spanish Empire was purely and solely an investment to pay for the home state, and not an area for pumping money into. However, in administering its empire the drain on Spain's manpower was great indeed: in his journal Woodes Rogers wrote that 'the Spaniards were always so jealous of this Commerce, that they wou'd never allow the least share of it to any other Nation, but oppos'd them with force whenever they attempted it'. He also noted that the inclination of the Spanish to keep their trade to themselves was so large that they used up their manpower to keep the trade flourishing and 'that in their Treaties with foreign Princes they were so very cautious as not to allow their ships so much as to touch on those Coasts but in extreme Necessity.'

Before the War of the Spanish Succession began, Spain's trade with the West Indies and its South American colonies ran in a direct route to Cadiz. From this city many other European nations traded with Spain, purchasing the treasures that had come from the Far East, and selling them on in their own countries. Rogers states that many English ships with English goods did business with Spain, sending their wares to Cadiz, which were then sent on to the Indies in return for valuable commodities such as gold and silver. A black market circumnavigated Cadiz and brought goods directly into English ports from Jamaica through the North Sea and Ireland. The black market flourished because privateers and merchants – Spanish included – were reluctant to pay the exorbitant sums the Spanish in Cadiz charged. If the Spanish caught any of these privateers, they would make a prize of any cargo they carried and imprison the crews or push them into slavery. Still, the privateers continued, largely because of the easier rates they could enjoy trading with England; and the Spanish trade that flourished between Panama and Peru and far down the Pacific Coast to Chile was also a tempting target for pirates and privateers.

In his journal, Rogers noted that the 1701 Grand Alliance saw the French usurp the crown of Spain, which led to Austria's forming an alliance with the Dutch and the English. 'That for the enlargement of navigation and commerce it should be lawful for us and the Dutch to seize by force what lands and cities we could of the Spanish dominions in America and to possess them as our own.' Before England could take advantage of the alliance, according to Rogers, the French got in first in a big way, sending two ships in 1698 from La Rochelle commanded by Admiral Beauchesne-Gouin into the South Seas to trade with the Spanish colonies. The admiral wrote a journal of his voyage and Rogers had a copy of it, an inspiration for him. From that point on, the French took full advantage of the trade, building their fleet up to seventeen French ships of war.

In 1697 Spain ceded to France the western half of the large island of Santo Domingo, now known as Haiti, one of the oldest of Spain's West Indies possessions. To govern this new French territory Governor and Admiral Jean-Baptiste du Casse, the Grand Monarque, was sent out and would become the dominant personality in the West Indies for some years. French-backed King Philip V of Spain increasingly relied on du Casse's naval forces to safely convoy the Spanish galleons and ships from the ports and colonies of the West Indies and the Caribbean to Spain. This made them 'absolute masters of all that valuable Trade which has enabled their Monarch hitherto to carry on the War against most of the Potenates of Europe which otherwise he could not have done,' as Rogers observed in his journal. Rogers also states that he was informed by some of the merchant ships they met or captured during his round-the-world voyage that French trade in the area had, in one year, amounted to more than 24 million pounds sterling.

A political man as well as a seafarer, Rogers believed that England had to make an extraordinary effort to build up trade in the South Seas in order to preserve the integrity of the nation. French involvement had dramatically reduced English trade between Spanish America and England. Rogers saw the rebuilding of trade with the Spanish colonies as vital if England was to keep its prosperity, and that one of the only ways of securing this prosperity was to seize some of those Spanish colonies and keep them for England.

At this time England's main enemy was France, ruled by Louis XIV and his puppet on the Spanish throne, King Philip V of Spain. The French, allied with Spain, were carrying all sorts of goods to Portobello, Vera Cruz, Carthagena, and Buenos Aires pushing England out of the trade they had previously enjoyed with the Spanish West Indies. Spanish ships would ply the Atlantic to the Caribbean where consignments for Peru would be taken by land because the route round Cape Horn at the foot of South America was forbidden by Spanish authorities – the waters were so perilous and dangerous that the Spanish did not want to risk losing their wealthy cargos in the violent seas. The result was that the Pacific waters were relatively unthreatened. Vital gold and silver came back to Spain through this route over the mountains from the great mines in Peru and Mexico. These precious metals went straight into the coffers of the Spanish Treasury in Seville. The Spanish fleet would assemble off Cartagena to pick up the goods brought from Panama or from the long mule trains that laboured over the foothills of the Andes through what is now Colombia. During war, the Spanish West Indian Fleet would convoy Spanish galleons along the coast of Central America to rendezvous with ships heading for Spain.

North of Panama, in the Pacific, Spanish galleons would sail from the Mexican port of Acapulco to the Philippines, returning loaded with oriental goods. Officially only two journeys a year were allowed for ships to go to Acapulco from Peru, where they would take on local goods rather than any of those goods brought from the Philippines.

South of Panama the Spanish colonial administration restricted trade and the number of voyages that could be undertaken in order to ensure that the richest cargo went to Old Spain. Under these restrictions a flourishing black market existed and many of the oriental goods brought in from the Philippines appeared in local shops in Peru and elsewhere because the Spanish governors and customs officials looked the other way as long as they were paid. In fact, there was a wide gap between the rules and their enforcement, largely because of the distance from Spain and within the vast Spanish colonies themselves but also because of corruption and a system that worked more on paper and did not take into account human failings.

Despite such corruption, the Spanish Indies were well integrated with Spain. For more than well over a century the bulk of the people were of Indian or mixed Indian and Spanish stock and had assimilated Spanish ways. In the Americas, West Indies and the Caribbean, Spanish viceroys ruled as representatives of the King of Spain in their own courtly splendour. It was under these viceroys that the government was structured, and all important government posts, with the exception of the local municipal posts, were held by men brought out from Spain. The same applied to the Church. It was rare indeed for one to find an Indian or native in any position of power, no matter how small.

There were two viceroys who represented King Philip of Spain. One was headquartered in New Spain, in Mexico City, the other in Lima. The viceroy in Mexico City had responsibility for the area from the Spanish West Indies, Florida and much of Spain's American colonies, while the viceroy in Lima covered an area from Chile to Panama to the east towards the River Plate. At this time, Lima rivalled many European cities for its splendour: with some 40,000 people the only city in England larger would have been London. Mexico City was also a true city of splendour and majesty as the viceroy was the highest overseas servant of the Spanish Crown and therefore earned the right to have his own court.

The Caribbean shores were the most susceptible to attack from buccaneers, pirates and privateers. The Pacific shores were safer, less liable to attack because fewer of Spain's enemies ever ventured to traverse the treacherous Cape Horn and sail into the Pacific. So when Rogers's little fleet appeared off the coast of Peru it caused a panic. The viceroys were responsible for the defence of their shores, for their settlements, their towns, villages, and their entire areas and defence was one of their most important concerns. A small Pacific squadron was at their disposal and ports such as Peru's Callao were fortified whenever the alarm was raised. If it was known that pirates or privateers were in the area, the alarm would be sounded, the defences on land strengthened and merchant ships armed with cannon. There was no standing army to speak of, except for the personal guard of the viceroy. Any soldiers needed were raised from the local population, quite often native Indians, black slaves or the American-born Spaniards and mixed Indian-Spanish natives. Against a small force of privateers this system worked; but against something much larger the far-flung settlements of Peru's viceroyalty were easy prey.

This was the state of the Spanish West Indies when Charles II of Spain died and the long War of the Spanish Succession began to see if the French-backed Bourbon King Philip V or Charles III would succeed him. Two important factors influenced politics at this time in the Spanish Americas; increasing French influence and control and the divided loyalties of the Spanish.

At the end of 1702 Philip had taken the throne, but the war continued. The two viceroys were the Duke of Albuquerque, a recent arrival in Mexico City (New Spain), and the Duke of Monclova, established in Lima for some considerable time. The latter's loyalty to the French-backed king was not as strong as it could have been, and his governors and subordinate officials thought the same way. They were lukewarm to the new French dynasty, whose grip on Spain itself was tightening while the campaign waged by the nations allied together against France descended into futility.

Slowly, new men were sent out to replace some of the official in the Spanish colonies, and these men were pro-French, if not French themselves. As Rogers states in his journal, the Spanish in the colonies disliked the French lording it over them and taking over the trade and their official posts. As French control mounted, news came to the British that many men in high positions in the Spanish Americas were more inclined to back the allied nominee for the Spanish Crown, Charles III or 'Don Carlos'. Indeed, in the early years of the war every effort was made by the allies to influence the authorities in the Spanish possessions to jump onto the 'Don Carlos' bandwagon.

Jamaica was a British possession and it was from here that a propaganda campaign was waged to influence those Spanish governors whose loyalty to the French king on the Spanish throne was wavering. The man directing this propaganda campaign was its governor, Thomas Handaside, and documents were sent out in 1705 and 1706 from Jamaica under the care of Rear Admiral Sir William Whetstone, Rogers's father-in-law. In the late spring of 1705 Whetstone was commanding the 70-gun *Suffolk* leading the West Indies squadron when he personally captured a French ship of war off Cartagena. Through the Spanish passengers and officers who had been taken prisoner from the French ship, Whetstone learned that the Spanish were 'weary of the French yoke and tyranny' and wanted to start trading with England again through Jamaica. He sent news directly back to England as quickly as he could. His letter was shown to Queen Anne, who instructed him to do all he could to sway more Spaniards and Spanish authorities in the Americas to the 'Don Carlos' cause.

Both Governor Handaside and Admiral Whetstone continued waging the political propaganda battle. A Spanish officer went ashore at Cartagena with declarations from Don Carlos promising that those who shook off the French shackles would be promoted. Whetstone and his ships lay off shore just to windward, waiting to see if the documents produced the hoped-for effect of uprising against the French. Nothing happened; so he left. But a few weeks later Whetstone was back off Cartagena and this time he saw a Spanish fleet of galleons ready to sail to Spain. He heard that du Casse was in the Carribean with a French fleet to act as convoy for the Spanish cargo ships. Stiffened by their stronger ally the Spaniards had failed to take the branch offered by the British even though they were largely unhappy with the pervasive presence of the French. The only thing that would sway the Spaniards would have been a superior English force, but as there was none there the political opportunity for the British was slipping away.

To make matters worse a new viceroy arrived from Spain, Don Manuel Omns de Santa Pau, Marques de Castelldosrius, a man held in high favour with King Philip V. Indeed, he had been the Spanish Ambassador in Paris and was now in Peru at the personal insistence of King Louis XIV, who dominated Spanish policy.

Spanish officials in Cartagena immediately gave trouble to the new viceroy, disliking his French attendants, and when the viceroy ordered the governor not to open the declaration sent to them by Whetstone, the governor ignored his request, opened the packet and sent some of its contents to Havana and Portobello as asked. By now the war in Spain was increasing. Don Carlos was said to be marching on Madrid; Whetstone conveyed this news to the Spanish officials when he was again off the coast of Peru.

By 1706 those fighting for the cause of Charles III were retreating after several disasters that left them holding only Catalonia. At the same time, a son was born to King Philip of Spain and this birth strengthened the hold of the Bourbons on the Spanish throne. News of the defeats by Charles III's allies and of the birth of the king's son simply served to consolidate loyalty to King Philip V.

Whetstone returned to his home in Bristol and more than likely became a huge influence on his son-in-law, the young Woodes Rogers, telling him of his exploits in the West Indies and encouraging him to head for the Pacific in search of gold, fame and fortune. As Rogers commented in his journal:

This Expedition being altogether new and of such vast consequence to our nation it ought to be adjusted with all the care and precaution possible; for I very much doubt, if our first attempt should miscarry, whether ever we should make a second.

Chapter 3

An Idea Takes Shape

Woodes Rogers had an idea and it was an idea that would not let go. It would do two things: it would hit at one of England's enemies, Spain, and it would quite possibly make him a rich man. The idea, we must assume, came from the books of the accounts of other mariners he had read and from the exploits of his father-in-law. Rogers had already sailed to far-off shores such as the islands of Madagascar and the fishery banks of Newfoundland. His plan was now to brave the fury of the waters around Cape Horn and sail into the Pacific to plunder and capture Spanish treasure. But there were difficulties and objections.

He wrote in his journal that there were four basic objections to his voyage, though he does not spell out where these came from. First, it would be too difficult for the ships to keep up with each other and that they would be strung out over too vast a distance; secondly, it would also be difficult to ensure there were enough stores and provisions for the outward and return journeys. A third objection was the improbability of having enough men to maintain a settlement or even find a site close to an already established colony that could supply the new settlement once the ships had gone back to England. The last major objection levelled against Rogers for his expedition was that they would not be able to set up trade in the new area nor be able to stop or interrupt French trade. And there was also Cape Horn to deal with.

Once Rogers set sail these objections were completely overcome, but in his journal he states that for the first objection his own experience and the experience of other seafaring men would keep ships in company for the voyage. Indeed, he made an entry in his journal stating that convoys of ships regularly ply the oceans from the East Indies back to Europe in company with each other.

Another objection dispelled was the issue of stores and provisions. Rogers states that 'our two ships were much fuller of men than usual for vessels of their burden and we carried provisions that served us sixteen months.' He makes the point that for every transport or military ship captured during the voyage that carried men another ship carrying mostly provisions would sail with the group as well, crewed by just enough men to sail her while the remaining space would be stocked with the provisions for the rest of the expedition. This meant that the 'victualler' ship could carry additional provisions for another ten months, more than enough for a return voyage to the South Seas.[3]

Scurvy was the main illness for such long voyages but by the time of Rogers's expedition the effects were well known and well provided for. Along the way the ships would refresh their supplies first at the Cape Verde Islands, then at Brazil. From Brazil to the South Sea is the longest part of the journey and includes traversing the Cape Horn at the tip of South America. In the early eighteenth century it would take ten weeks or so from Brazil to get to Chile, where the climate at that time was very beneficial so that those who were sick could quickly recover. 'Then as to proper places for settlement where provisions abound, there are so many of them on the coast of Chile that a well disciplined body of men under good commanders may settle there,' Rogers wrote.

The Spanish forces in these waters around Chile were so negligible that, according to Rogers, they could not properly put up a fight against a determined enemy. He wrote that there were three small Spanish ships and their land forces were not ready for war, as others before him had experienced. Additionally, the Chilean Indians were so averse to Spanish rule 'because of their Cruelty and Oppression that they readily joined the fairer English forces to throw off the yoke of oppression from the Spanish.'

Rogers then states that the only real enemy facing England was the French. By sea, Britain was superior, and Rogers was of the opinion that the English government who supported his expedition would take care to ensure its colonies and settlements were able to defend themselves. This rather naive outlook came to a head a few years later when, as Governor of the Bahamas, Rogers wrote several letters asking for help from the Royal Navy and the government to help him defend his territory against pirates and the Spanish. As we have seen in the Introduction, he received no reply from England.

It was his opinion that the government would do everything it could to remove the restrictions resulting from war in order to increase trade with the West Indies because he felt the people there were sick and tired of the French; once peace came the English government would be able to negotiate with Spain to lift the restraints the Spanish had placed on trading with their colonies in the West Indies. He firmly believed that whether there was war or peace the English could not trade in the region without settlements, which could either be negotiated during peacetime or taken by force during war. 'If King Philip continues to posses Spain and the Indies,' Rogers wrote, 'the French will still have as great an interest in Old Spain to make us trade there at a disadvantage.' Rogers passionately believed that, with the two crowns of Spain and France in the same family, and if King Philip was to gain full possession of Spain and the West Indies, Britain would be at a huge disadvantage when dealing with France. This 'Universal Monarchy' as he describes it would endanger the liberty of all of Europe. The likelihood of England setting up trade between Spain and the West Indies was, in his opinion, highly unlikely if a French monarch reigned in Spain. 'All our pretensions of trade to the South Sea unless settled in our possession during the war and confirmed by a peace are little to be depended upon.'

Turning to the actual voyage itself, Rogers states he would not have published his journal if his friends had not prevailed upon him to do so. He felt that publishers and the public, by the time his journal was published, expected journals of voyages to far distant shores should contain brand new discoveries of animals and people, whereas his was a voyage for which no such statement of fantastic animals or bizarre people would be found. But to appease the booksellers he did insert tales of far-off places, their history, their people and geography. Most of these come from people he had spoken to and places he had visited.

He talks about the high expectations of these undertakings that the actual truth of the voyage did not bear out. Indeed Rogers calls those buccaneers who 'set off on their own Knight Errantry and made themselves pass for prodigies of courage have given such romantic accounts of their adventures and told such strange stories that the voyages of those who come after look flat and insipid to unthinking people.' Perhaps he felt his own journal did not stand up to the fantastic tales of some who had gone before him because he urges the reader to look beyond amusement and understand that he was simply relating the truth

And the truth, in his journal, was this: he was to use just two ships, the *Duke* and the *Dutchess* suitably fitted out for the long cruise. These were two small frigates and the expedition was to be backed and paid for by several Bristol merchants.

To avoid troubles such as drunken indiscipline amongst the crews a written constitution was drawn up by the owners and signed by the officers of both ships. The expedition was run on a committee basis so that any action had to be decided in council first. Unfortunately, while the owners appointed Rogers 'first commander', they did not appoint him chairman of the committee. This post was held by Dr Thomas Dover, because he had one of the largest investments in the expedition. The owners thought that for this reason he would be the most willing to commit to action to make sure he recouped his investment. They were wrong.

On the *Duke*, the largest of the two frigates and where Rogers was captain, it included such men as Dover, Captain William Dampier, the pilot, the owner's agent, Mr Carleton Vanbrugh, Mr Green, the chief lieutenant, Mr Frye, the second lieutenant, with other officers listed as Mr Charles Pope, Mr Glendal, Mr Ballet and Mr Wasse. On the *Dutchess* the council was made up of Captain Stephen Courtney, his second captain, Cooke, the chief lieutenant Mr William Stretton and the owner's agent, Mr Bath, with officers Mr John Rogers and Mr White along with the master officers.

The idea behind having two councils was in case the ships should be separated from each other. Because Dover had one of the largest holdings it had been agreed that he should hold two positions of power and be in charge but that Rogers should have overall command of the running of the expedition and of all seafaring matters, unless there were any land operations where the Marines were needed, when Dover would take over. Whenever there was a major decision to be taken the constitution ordered that the officers must call a council and a swift decision be made by a majority vote. However, should there be any problems of discipline, differences or discontent, people could appeal directly to the captain (Rogers) or the President of the Council who could call a council for a hearing to decide on a course of action. The vote needed to be a majority and if the council was hung then Captain Dover had a double vote. This arrangement would prove to be a mixed blessing.

Throughout the voyage there were frequent councils in order for everyone to see that the officers who signed the decisions would carry them out. However, they did not have the power that the Royal Navy had aboard their ships for disciplining offenders. Rogers states that many punishments were mild and many disorders overlooked – there was insufficient power in any one hand to determine the difference between the officers. The only rules they had to follow were those provided by the ship owners.

In his journal Rogers wrote that he drew up every resolution and agreement, and so under extreme difficulties and far away from home he took on the command even though Captain Dover was titular head of the expedition. Dover was, as far as Rogers was concerned, third in command, 'according to the instructions given to me by our employers'.

***

During the years leading up to his expedition Rogers was involved in trading of different types. From 1705 to 1708 he was living in Bristol in Queen Square amongst the elite of Bristol merchant society. His first three children were born before he left for his voyage. In 1706 daughter Sarah, named after her mother, was born, and in January 1707 Rogers's first son, William Whetstone Rogers, was born and christened after his father-in-law, ending the Woodes tradition of naming the firstborn son after the father. We also know a girl named Mary was baptized in March 1708; it is unlikely that Rogers ever saw her again, since he set out shortly after her baptism and she died in 1712.

The Rogers's fortunes fluctuated during this three-year period. The deep sea trade from Bristol continued despite the war and the losses sustained from the war. Rogers too had losses at the hands of the French, which forced him to turn to privateering to make up for his failures in regular trading. In 1707 Rogers himself was backing privateers and sending them out with Letters of Marque that entitled them to attack French ships and seize French goods while paying a small proportion of their profits to the Crown. For example, a declaration was made in the Court of Admiralty on 18 February that Letters of Marque had been issued to Captain Henry Green, commander of a small privateer of sixteen guns and thirty men. The declaration identified the ship's owners as Woodes Rogers, Stephen Baker and Lewis Casamajor, a rich neighbour of Rogers's, while the ship was named the *Whetstone*. On 1 March Rogers's name again appears in a declaration when he and Baker backed a smaller ship of only eight guns and twenty men named the *Eugene Prize*, which was to set sail from the Avon with twenty small arms, twenty cutlasses, six powder barrels and one round per cannon. So Rogers's privateering had already begun before his dramatic voyage. He had also become a partner in the pottery works of Limekiln Lane.

In this period, privateering in home waters and even in the West Indies was common. Merchants and sailors alike were accustomed to mounting voyages from London and other ports. Sometimes the voyages would reap good riches but only occasionally since competition was fierce and the regular waters round England and the West Indies had been virtually cleared, while the waters in the Pacific were almost untapped.

Into this competitive marketplace came Woodes Rogers, whose aim for his voyage of the *Duke* and *Dutchess* was infinitely more ambitious than anything he had done before. He had his own losses to recover, and as his father-in-law,

Admiral Whetstone, was also out of work he too was looking for a profitable venture. Rogers needed to find ample financial support and with the help of Admiral Whetstone and the influential men of business and merchants he knew in Bristol he would get the backing needed for his momentous journey.

Rogers was inspired by the book by Beauchesne-Gouin about his voyage in 1698 to the Pacific. In 1703 three French merchantmen rounded the Horn and sailed into the Pacific, rendezvoused 300 miles west of Valparaiso at an island in the Juan Fernández group. There they ran into two English privateers under Thomas Stradling and William Dampier, who attacked one of the French ships, the *St Joseph*, without results. English prisoners were taken and the French sailed on to the Peruvian coast, where they began trading. After them came more French traders along with missionaries and others. So Rogers would have known how well the French were doing in the Pacific.

Filled with the ideas and experiences of Admiral Whetstone, this useful advice was something that no privateers in Bristol would be able to match. Indeed, the scale of the planning put every other expedition of the time well into the shade. Rogers's aim was to sail into the Pacific by way of the Horn to attack and create havoc, do damage and harass ships and the settlements of Peru. From there the voyage would continue up into Lower California, where the galleons that sailed from Manila to Mexico would be attacked and plundered. The way homeward would be not back the same way but across the Pacific and so round the Cape of Good Hope to England. Of course, to do this Rogers would need to have supplies and men to complete the voyage. However, there had to be a large investment to be sunk into the project before the ships ever left the dock.

We know that his backers were Sir John Hawkins, John Batchelor, James Hollidge, Christopher Shuter, Thomas Goldney and Francis Rogers. Three of them were to go on to be mayors of Bristol, Hawkins, Hollidge and Shuter. Shuter put up £3,105, the town clerk, John Romsey, £1,552; but the highest subscriber was Thomas Goldney, who put in £3,726. A leading businessman in the city of Bristol and a parishioner of St Nicholas, Alderman John Batchelor had since 1692 been deeply involved in privateering, starting out with the *Don Carlos* then sending out six other ships including the *Duke* and *Dutchess*. He purchased sixteen of the shares each at £103 10s to finance the equipment for the ships.

Both the *Duke* and the *Dutchess* were small frigates. The *Duke* was 320 tons with 36 guns, while the *Dutchess* was 260 tons with twenty-six cannon, only small guns which would prove to be a liability in serious action against much more powerful, well-armed vessels. By today's standards they would be considered small for the voyage and for the men and provisions they would have to carry to make that voyage a success. Their task was immense and the very lives of the officers and crews depended on the ships being able to carry the stores and the men for the entire journey. This is what makes his voyage so amazing. But the voyage was also fraught with personal problems and differences, as we shall see in later chapters.

Much of this dissent came from one corner, the President of the Council, Dr Thomas Dover, made captain by the owners only because he was one of the major backers, putting £3,312 into the venture but recouping some £423 per year as the chief medical officer for the journey. Dover had practised extensively in Bath and had a hot, overbearing temper. He was not new to the world of expeditions because he had made many to the West Indies. Including himself there were six people on the medical staff for the expedition; for example, Dover's brother-in-law was an apothecary and also doubled as lieutenant of landing parties. As Dover already had experience in expeditions is it reasonable to assume that he had some experience in military matters? At the one moment when the crew could have seized unimaginable wealth, Dover proved to be a coward, a lamb in wolf's clothing, a man of bluster and foolhardy temperament that would endanger the expedition. As we shall see later, it was he who decided to attack a ship three times the size of the *Dutchess*, a decision that cost the lives of more than twenty men.

One of the officers in the *Dutchess* was Woodes Rogers's younger brother, John. The second captain, or second-in-command and also another author who recorded the expedition was Edward Cooke. Like the others he had suffered losses at the hands of the French, having been captured twice in eight months and been stripped of his cargo. Both the agents who represented the owners were to look after all the plunder, making sure it was locked away, so that when it came to distribution, two-thirds went to the owners and a third was evenly distributed amongst the crew. However, both agents died on the voyage.

Other than Rogers himself, probably the most key individual was William Dampier. Most seafarers at that time were familiar with the waters around the Caribbean, or familiar with the Atlantic voyage across to the eastern seaboard of United States, but the Pacific was to many an unknown book. Dampier, already nationally known, was a man who had already sailed the Pacific and had put his adventures down on paper. His experience would prove to be priceless to Rogers. Twice he had sailed round the world, and in 1680 he had spent time on Juan Fernández Island. In his books, he provided details of winds and currents in the Pacific, of the trade winds which regularly blow off the coast of Peru and of the tides and currents of the South American rivers such as those around Guayaquil. With all this experience, Rogers and his backers engaged Dampier as the pilot for the expedition. Cooke states in his writings that during any council on the expedition Dampier's advice was always sought.

In his fifties, Dampier was now unlikely to be given a position of command, though he was still a fit man: according to Bryan Little, his last voyage to Australia, when he was in command, had proven to be a disaster. The position he was offered was not a comedown for him but had a twofold advantage: it was an honourable position because Rogers and his backers were respectable honest men, and of course it was a profitable position as well. Time and time again, Rogers and the rest of his crew were grateful to have the practical advice and experience of William Dampier.

Another individual of priceless importance to Rogers was Alexander White, the expedition's interpreter, although later he would prove to be not quite the blessing he appeared. White was invaluable to them whenever they came in contact with Spaniards or Spanish-speaking Indians. In addition, he had lived in Peru for some years, in the upland areas in the lands around the River Plate in what is now known as Bolivia. The information he imparted to Rogers on the territories and customs was essential and helped the expedition to build up trade with the local merchants in the area rather than blundering in as conquering heroes.

Slowly but surely preparations for the expedition got under way in the bustling and busy port of Bristol. The quay where the ships were tied up taking on stores for sixteen months in readiness for the voyage was packed with vessels plying the trade routes importing and exporting goods of all sorts. As the preparations progressed local people, shipbuilders, sailors, merchants, began to see that this was going to be no ordinary expedition. Speculation in the taverns and coffee-houses around the docks grew as people saw barrels of salt meat and flour being loaded into the ships' holds along with casks of ale and cider, and ammunition and powder being stowed in the magazines – far more than some thought necessary. Where were they going? Was it a round-the-world trip?

Finally, by the middle of summer 1708, the ships were ready to sail. They had been towed, by rowing boats, away from the quay clear of the River Avon out to the anchorage at King's Road where they lay with lighters, still continuing to load up stores and supplies. Finally, in August they raised their anchors. The expedition was on.

Chapter 4

The Voyage Begun

Gentlemen, as you did me the honour to approve my proposals for the following voyage and generously fitted out two ships, in which you gave me the principal command, I no sooner resolved to publish my journal: than I determined to choose you for my Patrons, and thereby to take an opportunity of expressing my gratitude to you, who had the courage to adventure your Estates on an undertaking which to men less discerning seemed impracticable. And I make no doubt it will be to your lasting Honour, that such a Voyage was undertaken from Bristol at your expense; since it has given the Publick a sufficient Evidence of what may be done in those Parts, and since the Nation has now agreed to establish a trade to the South Seas, which with the Blessing of God may bring vast riches to Great Britain. I wish you intire Health and happiness, and am, Gentlemen,

Your Most Humble Servant, Woodes Rogers

Both ships weighed anchor from King's Road, Bristol, on 22 August 1708 on the first leg of an amazing journey that would take the two small ships around the world. In company with the galleys *Prince Eugene*, *Berkely*, *Beecher*, *Sherstone* and the sloop *Diamond* along with the frigate *Scipio*, they moved away from the harbour and came to Minehead, where the little fleet anchored between ten o'clock and midnight before setting sail at six in the morning to catch a gale running past Minehead. The fleet was headed for Ireland.

In the late afternoon of the same day an attempt was made to add to the fleet when the *Dutchess* broke away 'like a young hound in chase of what seemed a larger ship which they lost sight of at 8 o'clock.'[4] Before leaving Bristol they had been informed that a French man-of-war was cruising in the waters between England and Ireland, so all that night the crews of the *Duke* and the *Dutchess* sailed with hammocks stowed, gun decks cleared, loose items locked away ready to fight.

On 5 August they parted company with the three galleys, including the *Prince Eugene*, and came to anchor at noon off two large rocks known as the

Sovereigns Bollacks[5] near Kinsale after overshooting their port. By eight that evening they took advantage of a light easterly gale and weighed anchor. Onboard with Rogers was a pilot from Kinsale who turned the small fleet into the next bay west of Cork, when the weather was dark and foggy. 'Which,' Rogers wrote in his journal, 'provoked me to chastise him for undertaking to act as pilot without understanding his business better.'

Two days later the *Duke* and *Dutchess* entered the cove of Cork and anchored there to shelter from the weather which was so poor it kept them there until 28 August. Rogers noted that the weather that day was fine enough to 'careen, clean and tallow the ships five streaks below the water line'.[6] Indeed, no privateer worth his salt would allow the bottom of his ship not to be perfectly clean. Rogers himself was never happier than when he had both ships almost on their beam ends with the keel nearly out of the water for scraping and cleaning the bottom.

At this time we can see Rogers's foresight, for he ensured that both ships doubled up on their officers. 'We now have double the number of officers usual in privateers,' he wrote. 'Besides a large compliment of men. We took this method of doubling our offices to prevent muntinies, which often happen in long voyages and that we might have a large provision for a succession of officers in each ship in case of mortality.'

While taking on supplies and stores at Cork during this layover, Rogers noted some strange behaviour amongst some of the men. 'They were continually marrying whilst we staid there though they expected to sail immediately.'[7] Amongst the complement of men there was a Dane who married an Irish girl, though neither could speak the other's language and had to communicate through an interpreter. Yet Rogers perceived this pair to be the most upset when they set sail, with the young Dane very sad for several days after they had left Cork.

We have already seen the make-up of the officers of each of the ships, with very few of them being able to claim any connection to sailing, though most of them had some form of connection to the backers or had invested money in the ships. We already know that Thomas Dover was second captain of the *Duke* and captain of the Marines and that he had little or no experience in military matters or seamanship, since he was a doctor. His first lieutenant was a relation, one Mr Hopkins, who was an apothecary.

But the crew were a wide variety of different individuals. There were the boatswains, gunners, carpenters and those one would expect to find on ships rigged for long sea voyages. 'A third were foreigners,' Rogers wrote. 'While of

Her Majesty's subjects many were tailors, tinkers, pedlars, fiddlers and hay-makers, with ten boys and one negro: with which mixed gang we hope to be well manned as soon as they have learnt the use of arms, and got their sea legs: which we doubt not soon to teach 'em and bring 'em to discipline.'

Finally, on 1 September, the *Duke* and the *Dutchess* raised anchor and sailed out of the cove of Cork with twenty other merchant vessels under convoy by HMS *Hastings*. Both ships were very crowded and overloaded with provisions and so encumbered with cables between their decks that they were completely unfit to fight an action against any other ships without having to throw overboard most of their supplies. Yet despite this, the following day, both the little frigates left the fleet to chase a sail they had sighted to windward. This was more of a test of their fighting and sailing ability, and Rogers was pleased with their performance. 'We begin to hope we shall find our heels, since we go so well tho' deep and pestered.'

With fine weather on 4 September, Rogers and Captain Courtney of the *Dutchess* received a signal from Captain Paul of the galley *Sherstone*. Both captains were rowed across to the other vessel where they were joined by the commander of the *Scipio*. It was here that Captain Paul proposed joining them off the coast of Cape Finisterre for a few days of privateering, for the area was known to have rich pickings. Shortly after they rowed back from the *Sherstone* to their respective vessels, Rogers knew it was time to part company with HMS *Hastings*. 'It became necessary,' he wrote, 'to acquaint the ships companies with our desinges in order that while in company with one of Her Majesties ships any malcontents might be exchanged into her.' Luckily for Rogers there were none. However, parting at that time with the *Hastings* meant that the little cruise planned for Cape Finisterre had to go by the board. Signalling to Captain Paul, Rogers saluted and Paul replied by wishing both ships a prosperous journey.

'The wind North by West and clear weather,' Rogers wrote as they set sail across the Bay of Biscay. This was the first time that Rogers put an entry into his journal about the first dinner onboard his ship with the officers of the *Dutchess*. They returned the favour the following day; and so this constant interaction between the officers of both the little frigates went on. Few days passed at sea without some form of communication between the two ships by boat. The lowering and hoisting of lifeboats[8] for rowing the various officers across from one ship to another gave the crews some very practical experience,

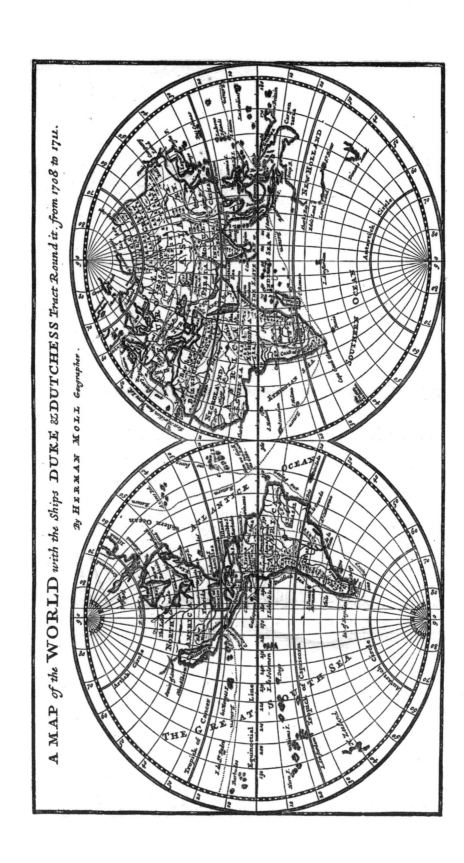

A MAP of the WORLD with the Ships DUKE & DUTCHESS Tract Round it: from 1708 to 1711.

By HERMAN MOLL Geographer.

even when a high sea was running. There is no record of any mishap or loss of life to the boat crews throughout the voyage, a testament to the seamanship they learned while on the voyage.

Without a doubt Rogers was the leader of this expedition, although Dover, as President of the Council, was nominally in charge. Both ships formed a loose federation and no important decisions were taken without the officers of both coming together in council or committee meetings. The first parliament held by the officers was to consider the length of the voyage. 'The many different climates we must pass, and the excessive cold which we cannot avoid going about Cape Horn; at the same time we have but a slender stock of liquor and our men are meanly clad, yet good liquor to sailors is preferably to clothing.' This entry in Rogers's journal was marking the first time the committee sat on the *Duke* to decide if a stop should be made at Madeira. The men present at this meeting were Thomas Dover (President), Stephen Courtenay, Woodes Rogers, Edward Cooke, William Dampier, Carleton Vanbrugh, Thomas Glendall, John Bridge, John Balley and Robert Frye.

The following morning at six a sail was sighted in the distance and both ships gave chase, with the *Dutchess* a mile in the lead. The sea was high with large swells and both the frigates bore down on the distant sail, gradually chasing her. Sailing to windward it took them nine hours to catch up with the other ship, which showed Swedish colours. The *Dutchess* fired a volley of cannon fire at the ship and then the *Duke* fired another. 'She brought to, when we boarded her; Captain Courtney's boat being just before ours,' Rogers wrote. 'We examined the master and found he'd come round Scotland and Ireland.'

This route was used by many ships of different nationalities at the time to avoid being captured by the British in the Channel. This choice of route made Rogers suspect that the Swede had something to hide and therefore could be their first prize. Some of the crew of the Swedish vessel told him they had gunpowder and cables onboard. That was enough. Rogers decided to investigate further and left twelve men onboard while he took the Swedish master and twelve of his men back to the *Duke* for further questioning. In the end he had to let her go as nothing was found to prove her to be a prize. They parted with gifts being exchanged on both sides. The Swedish captain gave Rogers two hams and some dried beef, while Rogers provided a dozen bottles of cider.

While he was onboard the Swedish vessel some of his own men mutinied under the leadership of the boatswain and three junior (inferior as Rogers refers to them) officers. But with his chief officers behind him, the ringleaders were confined in irons. Ten in all were confined this way, and one of them was whipped first for insisting the others join him in the mutiny. The reason for the uprising, which was very small to begin with, was that some of the crew were unhappy about not plundering the Swedish vessel. They thought that regardless of her cargo that they should not have let her go, according to Rogers. But he had bigger fish in mind.

'On September 14th a sailor, followed by near half the ship's company came after to the steeridge door, and demanded the boatswain out of irons,' Rogers wrote. 'I desired him to speak with me on the quarter deck, which he did, where, the officers assisting, I tied him up and made one of his chief comarades whip him, which method I thought best for breaking any unlawful friendship amongst themselves.'

Rogers stated in his journal that he believed the mutiny could not have been so easily put down if it was not for the large number of officers (over thirty-six) onboard. After the whipping the mutineers and the crew quietly submitted. Two days later, the mutineers were set free, after humbly submitting to Rogers's authority and promising good behaviour.

On 18 September 1708, the little fleet was off Pico Tenerife, where they captured their first prize. At five o'clock the next morning, they picked up a sail some distance off their lee bow and altered course to chase it. Turning to bring the wind into his sails Rogers barked his orders at the crew as they gave chase. Rogers was a meticulous sailor, always making sure that the hull of the *Duke* was as clean as it could be and that his ship was rigged for the fastest running possible, for in most cases he was able to catch up with his prey. Drawing closer to the mystery ship they soon discovered it was a Spanish vessel of about 25 tons. Boarding their new prize, Rogers and the rest of his party found out that the ship was sailing for the island of Fuerteventura with forty-five passengers onboard. 'They rejoiced when they found us English,' Rogers wrote, 'because they feared we were Turks.'

This prize was at first a headache for Rogers, but in the end proved to be a windfall. For at this stage while they were at the Grand Canaries, Rogers's chief concern was to ensure that both ships had enough liquor and stores for the voyage around Cape Horn. The Spanish vessel had a cargo of two butts of wine and a hogshead of brandy, which would have been enough but for the agent onboard the *Duke,* Carleton Vanbrugh, who decided to go ashore with the master of the Spanish ship to negotiate its ransom. He was of course immediately imprisoned and the authorities sent a message to Rogers demanding the release of the Spanish ship free of charge, claiming protection from capture of all vessels trading between the Canary Islands. This was supported not only by the British Consul at Orotava but also by some English merchants who lived and worked in the Canaries and who sent Rogers a letter advising him to give up the captured Spanish ship.

Rogers's reply was short and to the point. Possession, he claimed, was nine-tenths of the law. The Spanish authorities replied demanding the immediate release of the prisoners and the ship. Rogers sent a quick dispatch saying he would wait until morning for their answer. Meanwhile he would cruise among the islands making reprisals and by eight in the morning he would visit the town of Orotava with his guns ready to sink any vessels there, especially the Governor's ship, and bombard the town. 'This letter,' Rogers wrote in his journal, 'had the desired effect for as we stood in close to the town at eight o'clock next morning, we spy'd a boat coming off, in which proved to be one Mr. Crosse, an English merchant and our agent Mr Vanbrugh with wine, grapes, hogs, and other necessaries for the ransom of the bark.' Once the boat was alongside, they immediately began loading its cargo between their two ships and handed the Spanish prisoners back to Crosse along with whatever possessions of theirs they could find.

The work over, Rogers sailed away happy. 'Now we are well stocked with liquors we shall be better able to endure cold when we get the length of Cape Horn,' he entered in his journal.

Late in the afternoon of 22 September, in a high sea, the *Duke* spotted a sail to their westward and the two ships chased it until a strong gale forced them to abandon the chase.

They encountered fine weather the following day with fresh gales and once again the officers dined together on the *Duke* where a committee was held to discuss the disciplining of Vanbrugh who had acted against Rogers's wishes. An old seafaring tradition for sailors who crossed the Equatorial Line was ducking. It was decided that Vanbrugh would be the first to be ducked into the sea several times. Rogers observed that the ducking was done by putting a rope through a block from the main yard-arm to hoist the person halfway up to the yard where the rope was let go so they could fall into the water. A stick was crossed through their legs and well fastened to the rope for the sake of safety. 'This proved to be of great use to our freshwater sailors to recover the colour of their skins which were grown very black and nasty,' Rogers recorded in his journal. While Vanbrugh was the first to be ducked many others were ducked as well, upwards of sixty according to Rogers. Most of them were sent into the water three times but others were ducked up to twelve times. Presumably this was to boast about on their return to England, with some of the crew going for the ducking championship title of the voyage, no doubt, for Rogers actually stated this was 'the better title for being treated when they come home'.

On 29 September the *Duke* and the *Dutchess* arrived at the Cape Verde Islands, off the coast of West Africa, and sailed through the night west and west by north heading for St Vincent. 'We were going by easy sail all night because we had none aboard either ship that was acquainted with these islands.' On 30 September they arrived at St Vincent and anchored in the bay.

One thing we must remember here is that there were no computers or electronic navigation aids or even detailed charts for mariners to navigate by in those days. In many cases they used dead reckoning for their longitude; so the accuracy of the landfalls that Rogers made and the boldness of his navigation is truly surprising. Their charts were very limited. They would have had a version of the Davis Quadrant but probably not a sextant.

While at St Vincent Rogers and his party began to take on water and other supplies: 'We cleared our ships, but it blowed too hard to row our boatloads of empty butts ashore; and we could do little to wooding and watering till this morning. We were forced to get a rope from the ship to the watering-place, which is a good half mile from our anchorage and so hauled our empty casks ashore by boatloads in order to have 'em burnt and cleaned in the inside.'

A boat was sent to St Antonia with the linguist Joseph Alexander aboard, with a letter to the governor asking for supplies, for although the people of the island were poor they still had plenty of cattle, goats, hogs, fowls, melons, potatoes, limes, brandy and tobacco. The letter stated that they could not stay for more than a couple of days and that the bearer of the letter, Alexander, would be able to tell the governor of all the occurrences taking place in Europe and the great successes against the French and Spanish, which should speed a lasting peace. However, two days later Rogers entered into his journal that the boat had returned with two cattle, one for each ship, but without Alexander. Whether the linguist had met with a worse fate that Vanbrugh had done when he went ashore at the Canaries and was detained or had just decided to get off the ship and not return, little is known; but Rogers simply wrote this note in the margin of his journal – 'our linguist deserts.'

In a hastily convened committee meeting the officers quickly decided not to stay to wait for Alexander but to continue on their voyage. From this committee arose a debate about preventing mutinies and disorders amongst the crew, who were unhappy about the Spanish bark they had taken off the Canaries. The crew wanted to keep the bark whereas Rogers wanted the supplies they could get for it, which was why it was ransomed and given back.

The committee decided to set up some rules regarding plunder taken from captured ships. The plunder was first to be judged as plunder by the senior officers and agents aboard each ship, and anybody who concealed plunder twenty-four hours after the prize was taken was to be severely punished and would forfeit his share. Any seaman who was drunk and disorderly during battle or who disobeyed his officers' orders would also meet the same punishment. Public books of plunder were to be kept in each ship and the plunder was to be appraised and divided as soon as possible after it was captured. Also, every person was to be searched when they came onboard and those who refused lost their share of the loot. It was also agreed that the whole cabin plunder was to be divided amongst the crew and that Captains Rogers and Courtney were to have 5 per cent over and above their standard shares. Further, a reward was to be given to anyone who first saw a prize of not less than 50 tonnes.

This agreement was made in order to bring some sort of peace amongst the crew and the officers. 'Without which we must unavoidably have run into such continual scenes of mischief and disorder,' Rogers recorded in his journal, 'which have not only tended to the great hindrance, but generally to the total disappointment of all voyages of this nature, that have been attempted so far abroad in the memory of man.'

On 8 October 1708 the *Duke* and *Dutchess* raised their anchors and at seven in the evening sailed away from St Vincent after putting ashore the Deputy Governor of St Antonio, whom they had been entertaining. In his journal Rogers described the islands as having very large spiders whose webs were so strong that it was difficult to get through them. 'The heats are excessive to us newly arrived from Europe, so that several of our men began to be sick and were blooded.' Some of the officers decided to go ashore to hunt and found wild ass as the only game on the islands. They gave a long chase and finally got within range of a shot but were unable to bring the beast down and it disappeared into the undergrowth. The officers returned to their ships empty-handed, hot and weary.

As the ships got further and further away from England they turned increasingly towards prayer, reading in both ships in the evening and in the morning every day in accordance with Church of England doctrines. Despite this, there were problems not only with the crew but also with junior officers. Rogers's first method to relieve problems with these men was to shift the junior officers from ship to ship, but on one occasion after a dinner onboard the *Dutchess* on 22 October, Captain Courtney went aboard the *Duke* with his second-in-command, Captain Cooke, ordering him to get his second mate, Mr Page, who was to be exchanged with Mr Ballett. Page, however, did not want to change. Before going over to the *Duke*, Page refused to get into the boat from the *Dutchess* and was struck by Captain Cooke for disobeying orders. Page, ignoring protocol, immediately struck the officer back and both men fought hard, exchanging several blows before Page was finally subdued, tied up and put into the *Dutchess*'s boat and rowed over to the *Duke*. Once onboard that ship Page was ordered into the bilboes, long steel bars with shackles that slid up and down with a lock at the end. These were used to confine the feet of prisoners in the same way as handcuffs would be for confining a person's hands.

The wily Page, however, did not manage to get into the bilboes. Telling his guard, a corporal, that he was desperate to use the head the corporal left him for a while, and Page dove over the side of the *Duke* into the smooth calm sea to swim back to the *Dutchess* while the two captains were onboard the *Duke*. However, the boat from the *Dutchess*, still alongside the *Duke*, began rowing after him and soon overtook him. Roughly plucked out of the water by the boat men they turned the boat around and rowed back to the *Duke* where Page was taken aboard and lashed. Swearing loudly and cursing, he tried to get away again; so Rogers decided to lock him into irons.

A week later, after swearing he would behave appropriately from that moment on, Rogers had Page released. Two days after that, on 2 November 1708, two members of the expedition were put into the bilboes for stealing part of the plunder taken from the Spanish bark (ship) – two shirts and a pair of stockings. 'After which,' Rogers wrote, 'they beg'd pardon, promis'd Amendement and were discharged.'

In his journal, Rogers recorded a tornado with lightning that lasted upwards of an hour, and came down on them as 'if it had been liquid'. Apart from this storm nothing remarkable is recorded about the voyage after leaving the Cape Verde Islands until 16 November when, with a fair wind from the east, both ships arrived off what they supposed was the island of Cape Frio on the Brazilian coast. The wind then failed and they found themselves in foggy, rainy weather. Hoisting their boats into the sea, the men rowed in front of the frigates while men at the bow of each ship threw ropes to the men in the boats.

For two days they towed and rowed the ships on their course, using the boats from both the frigates until they were finally able to anchor in a cove off the Isle de Grande, where they decided to bring onboard wood, water and other supplies and to careen their ships.

On 21 November, at six o'clock after the torrential rain of the afternoon had died away, Rogers sent the pinnace from the *Duke* with Captain Cooke and Lieutenant Pope to the village of Angre de Reys, about three leagues from their position, to notify the governor of the island that they had arrived and to give him gifts of butter and cheese. The aim was to gain the governor's friendship should any of their men run away. Earlier that afternoon, Captain Courtney of the *Dutchess* had put eight men in irons for disobeying orders.

As the little boat approached the town several shots were fired at them from the shore. Ducking down in the boat they continued their approach. Suddenly the firing stopped and slowly Cooke and Pope peered over the edge of the gunwhale to see what was happening. No more shots came their way so both commanders, much more confident, pushed their crews forward. The reason the firing had stopped was because the people on the shore realized that they were not French boats. 'The Fryars invited them to the Convent, and told them they were often plundered by the French or they should not have been so ready to fire at 'em,' Rogers recorded in his journal. Because the French had treated them so badly, the Portuguese natives were suspicious of everyone approaching their town. Both Cooke and Page discovered also that the governor was away and they returned to the *Duke* just before midnight the same day. While they were out, some of the men cast the fishing nets from the *Duke* and *Dutchess* into the cove where Rogers says they caught some very good fish.

At the same time the main and fore masts, what Rogers refers to as 'Trusle-Trees' of the *Duke*, were taken down to be repaired. He sent their carpenter ashore with a Portuguese guide to search for the appropriate wood for the masts but the torrential rain forced them to abandon the mission. 'While so engaged we found abundance of Frenchmen's graves,' Rogers wrote. The Portuguese told them these were the graves of sailors from two very large French ships; almost half the crews of both ships had succumbed to the tropical heat while they had watered at the cove. French ships watered there on their way homeward or to the South Seas. 'This morning we had several canoes from the town with limes. Fowls, Indian corn etc. to exchange for such things as we could spare. We treated 'em all very civilly and offered a gratuity to such as would secure our Men if any of 'em run away: they all promised to give us good information and assist us in searching after 'em.'

The weather was intolerably hot to the Europeans and yet they decided to clean one side of the *Dutchess* on the afternoon of the 24th and careened the other side the following morning. This was done by attaching rope and tackle to the masts of the ship to be cleaned. The tackle and rope was attached to the other ship's hull and the ship to be cleaned was then hauled down to forty-five degrees. All the shot and stores had to be taken out and put into the other ship while this cleaning took place.

It must have been exhaustive work, especially in the tropical heat. Rogers wrote an interesting entry into his journal for that day as he let the boat from the *Duke* go ashore with several officers and men for a short spell of leave, telling them they had to be back by noon because they would then need the boat. The party did indeed return by noon, but had brought with them a giant animal. 'They brought with 'em a monstorous creature, which they'd killed, having prickles like a hedgehog, with fur between them and a head and tail like a monkey's. It stank intolerably which the Portuguese told us was only the skin, that the meat of it was very delicious and that they, the Portuguese, often killed them for the table.' But none of the men had the stomach for skinning the beast and trying it out, so the creature was thrown over the side to save the nasal passages of everyone onboard.

On 26 November, Michael Jones and James Brown, whom Rogers labelled as Irish landmen, quietly slid over the side of the *Duke* and swam ashore, running into the woods to get away from the rest of the expedition 'in spite of the experiences of two such sparks that ran away the day before from the *Dutchess* . . . In the night they were so frighted with tigers as they thought, but really by monkeys and baboons, that they ran into the water hollering to the ship till they were fetched aboard again.' However, on the day the two Irish landmen escaped, a canoe was seen heading away from the ship. Officers and men onboard the *Duke* were now suspicious and called for the canoe to stop; no response came from the friar and the Indians manning the canoe. Rogers, suspecting the canoe of either grabbing the two Irish landmen or coming to get them off the ship, ordered the pinnace to be sent out after the canoe. The pinnace hit the water and its crew began rowing hard after the canoe. Drawing closer to the other vessel the *Duke*'s agent, Vanbrugh, ordered the men in the pinnace to fire on the canoe. A shot was fired across its bow but the canoe continued onwards, so Vanbrugh ordered shots to be fired into the canoe itself, until one of the Indians was wounded. 'He was the property of a certain fryar who owned and steered that canoe,' Rogers entered in his journal. The friar had a quantity of gold which Rogers supposed came from the mines where he had been saving souls. The friar alleged that the amount was £200 and that not only had he lost his gold when he landed on the beach of the little wooded island where they got their wood for the masts, but he had also lost his slave.

When the canoe landed, the wounded Indian was unable to move so he was taken back to the *Duke* where his wound was dressed by the ship's surgeon, but he died two hours later. 'I made the Father as welcome as I could but he was very uneasy at the Loss of his Gold and the Death of his Slave and said that he would seek for justice in Portugal or England.'

The next day, 27 November, the *Dutchess* weighed anchor and was towed about a mile out of the cove where it anchored to wait for the *Duke*. Their boats returned again to the cove and spied two men waiting under the trees on the little wooded island by the shore, hoping for a Portuguese canoe to take them off. The boats landed on each side of the point, unseen by the two men. Stealthily moving through the woods to the two men waiting, the little force captured the two waiting men without firing a shot. They turned out to be the two Irish landmen. 'I ordered them both to be severely whipped and put in chains,' Rogers wrote.

Two days later a committee was convened on the *Dutchess* while they were still off the Isle de Grande. This committee was to decide the fate of Vanbrugh who, in firing upon the canoe three days earlier and mortally wounding the Indian had disobeyed Rogers's direct orders. He could no longer be allowed to stay aboard the *Duke*. Both Rogers and Courtney presided over this committee as it was a matter of discipline and therefore came under the jurisdiction of Rogers rather than Thomas Dover, President of the Council. The first part of the committee was a statement acknowledging that since they had captured the first prize off the Canary Islands they had had to sell some of the prize to purchase liquor and other necessities for the men for the journey round Cape Horn. 'They being very meanly clothed and ill provided to endure the Cold and we have and do hereby desire the Agent of each ship to take particular Cognizance of what such goods are sold and disposed of,' the minutes of the meeting recorded. The committee then turned to the incident of 26 November when Vanbrugh shot the Indian. The statement goes over the facts of the case that a canoe coming near the *Duke* as she rode anchor at the island of Grande on the Brazilian coast. Men from the *Duke* hailed the canoe, which did not respond. They hailed her again and the canoe rowed away. 'The Captain ordered the Boat to get ready and pursue her. And Mr Carleton Vanbrugh,

Agent of the said Ship, putting of the Boat without the Order of his Captain, or before any Commanding Officer was in pursuit of her, fired or ordered to be fired, at her federal muskets at a distance.' The statement continues that as the boat drew closer Vanbrugh ordered the men to fire into the boat which killed the Indian. The rest of the statement describes the padre, the dead Indian's master, and the £200 he had lost, 'which he says he carry ashore and hid in hopes to preserve which could not be aftwards found also, he says he does verily believe it was not taken by any of the Ships company but alledges it was lost by means of their chasing and surpising him.'

They then made a written protest against Vanbrugh's actions because he had proceeded without any orders from the captain and for acting against what he was on the voyage for – namely to be the agent for the owners of the *Duke*. The committee then decided 'to remove Mr Carleton Vanbrugh from being Agent of the *Duke* Frigate to be agent of the *Dutchess* and to receive Mr William Bath Agent of the *Dutchess* in his place.'

Their stay at Isle de Grande ended on a high note as they took part in a religious festival at Angre de Reys where the governor, Senior Raphael de Silva Lagos had returned. With a party of ten including musicians, two trumpets and an hautboy,[9] they marched in procession to the town's little church. According to Rogers, they played several 'noisy paltry tunes' with everyone singing. After services were read, the procession marched out with the musicians at the head with an old father and two friars next to them carrying incense with about forty priests, followed by the governor of the town, Rogers and Captain Courtney. Both Courtney and Rogers carried long wax candles. After the two-hour ceremony, 'we were splendidly entertained by the fathers of the Convent and then by the Governor.'

Rogers reciprocated the entertainment the following day by inviting the governor and the friars onto the *Duke*. After the friars had given toasts to the pope, Rogers to the Archbishop of Canterbury and others, the governor and the friars spent the night onboard the frigate as the weather turned with thick showers and high winds. The following morning their guests left the *Duke*. 'We made them a handsome present of butter and cheese from both ships in consideration of the small presents and yesterday's favours.'

In his own journal Rogers entered his observations of Brazil. He was well versed in the Spanish, Portuguese and Dutch voyages of the sixteenth and seventeenth centuries, so he already had an idea of what he would find. 'The natives of Brazil live in huts built of stakes and covered with Palm leaves,' he wrote. 'Their dishes and cups are calabashes or the shells of a sort of pompion, their furniture is hammocks of cotton-like net-work, these they use for beds when they travel, tying them to trees.' He continues that the women follow their husbands into war and everywhere else, carrying their luggage in baskets while also carrying the babies in 'a peece of calico, a parrot or an ape in one hand; while the idle lubber carries nothing but his arms.' He continued by saying that the way they counted the years was by laying out a chestnut in each season. As far as their religion was concerned they believed they were turned into demons if they did nothing with their lives while those who killed and ate their enemies, according to Rogers, would find all sorts of pleasures in beautiful fields and mountains.

Chapter 5

An Amazing Discovery

As 1708 came to a close and the little frigates left the Isle de Grande, their next stop to resupply, take on stores and refresh was at Juan Fernández, off the coast of Chile, some 6,000 miles away. However, first they had to circumnavigate Cape Horn, the southernmost tip of South America and one of the most treacherous waterways in the world. Knowing how far they had to travel before taking on more supplies they made sure they had enough for the long, hazardous journey ahead.

On 3 December they cleared the Brazilian coast. Three days later, Rogers recorded in his journal that an albatross came through the fog and flew away.[10] He says it had a wingspan of eight to ten feet. On 7 December the rain blew in gales from the east, accompanied by thunder and lightning – a frightening scene. But for Rogers it was business as usual as he removed one of the boatswain's mates and replaced him with Mr Hollanby, one of their best sailors by Rogers's account.

Three days later he exchanged another boatswain's mate, Benjamin Long, with Thomas Hughes of the *Dutchess*, who was 'being mutinous there, they were willing to be rid of him.' On 13 December the gales began to come in from the south-west, forcing Rogers to reef the mainsail,[11] the first time they had to do so since leaving England. As they sailed on Rogers remarked on the cold. 'It is much colder in this latitude,' he wrote. 'It is 43.30 South than in the like degrees north though the Sun was in its furthest Extent to the southward, which may be ascribed partly to our coming newly out of the warmer climates.' The other reason for the cold, Rogers wrote, was that he thought the wind was blowing over larger tracts of ice than in the same degrees north.

Either way, the weather was getting worse as they approached Cape Horn.

On one occasion they experienced thick fog and lost sight of the *Dutchess* but by making noises that the captains had previously agreed between them should such a thing happen they were able to communicate. On 18 December the weather was so cold and hazy that one of the men on the mizzen mast of the *Dutchess* fell and landed on the deck below, suffering a severe head wound. Hearing of the accident, Rogers came aboard with two surgeons to see what could be done, but neither surgeon could do anything, and the man died. They buried him at sea the next day.

At ten o'clock on the morning of 23 December they sighted land some south-south-east distant, appearing first as three islands then as several more islands. 'We saw most of that which appeared to be first islands, join with the low lands.' These islands were what is known today as the Falkland Islands or, as Rogers put it, 'Falkland's Land, described in a few draughts, and none lay it down right, though the Latitude agrees pretty well.'

Christmas Day 1708 saw the two ships sailing under a strong wind blowing in from the south-west and by six in the evening they had lost sight of the Falklands though did catch sight of a distant sail under their lee bow. Immediately, Rogers ordered the sails to be let out and gave chase. He brought the *Duke* round but by ten that night they had lost sight of the the sail. 'We spoke our consort and agreed to bear away to the northward till dawn, as we were both of opinion that if homeward bound the chase after losing sight of us, would steer north.'

But the next morning the weather was thick and hazy and they saw nothing; only when the weather cleared did they catch sight of the distant sail on the horizon. By now the weather was calm and the wind had died away. Both ships got their oars out and gave chase. Rowing and towing the ships with their boats they slowly gained on the distant sail. Around six that evening, they were approaching the ship and Rogers rowed over to the *Dutchess* to speak with Captain Courtney 'to agree how to engage her if a great ship, as she appeared to be, and adjusted signals, if either of us should find it proper to board her in the night.' By the time Rogers had left the *Dutchess* and returned to the *Duke*, the wind had sprung up again. Rogers ordered the sails to be raised, making all possible haste to keep up the chase. However, by the time darkness came at ten that night the weather was again hazy, making visibility very difficult. 'Being short nights, we thought it impossible to lose one another,' Rogers wrote. With the *Dutchess* off their starboard bow Rogers decided to shorten the sail around one in the morning in case they lost sight of the *Dutchess*.

The morning of 27 December saw thick fog again and neither the *Dutchess* nor the ship they were chasing was visible. An hour later, the fog cleared. 'We saw our consort on our larboard bow and fired a gun for her to bear down, but we immediately saw the chase ahead of the *Dutchess* a few miles, which gave us new life.' The wind was now almost directly ahead of them as they chased the unknown ship a few miles ahead of the *Dutchess*. Indeed, Rogers was pushing the *Duke* to catch up with the *Dutchess* ahead of him. But the water was smooth and though they 'ran at a great rate' they were unable to catch up with the *Dutchess*, who was also unable to keep up the chase. 'The chase outbore our consort so she gave off,' wrote Rogers. 'Being to windward came down very melancholy to us.'

Rogers suspected the ship of being a French homeward bound ship from the South Seas.[12] However, at the time of the chase Rogers was concerned that the ship had outrun them. Nor did he know why they had sighted the ship where they had, since most ships stayed within sight of the Falklands heading home or for the South Seas. Although his own ships were clean and sailing well, very few English ships of the time were able to outrun the French ships built for trade or for piracy in the South Seas.

On New Year's Eve they struggled against high winds, gales and rain. Despite the weather, the following morning, New Year's Day 1709, Rogers had a large tub of hot punch put on the quarterdeck and the *Duke*'s officers wished every man onboard a Happy New Year to the music played by the ship's musicians. 'Every man in the ship had above a pint to his share and drank our owners and friends' health in Great Britain, to a happy New Year, a good voyage and a safe return.' They then headed towards the *Dutchess* and, coming in close, the crew of the *Duke* gave the *Dutchess* three 'huzzas' and wished them all a Happy New Year.

Throughout the three-year voyage the *Duke* and *Dutchess* sustained remarkably little damage from high seas and storms. But now, as they approached the Horn, they were about to go through their worst part of the voyage yet. On 5 January 1709 they were in the leg of the voyage round Cape Horn when the weather turned nasty. High seas blown by the worst gales they had yet encountered threw the ships around the rough seas, waves and spray crashing across their decks. Bracing himself against the railing of the bridge Rogers ordered the foresail and mainsail to be reefed, and by six o'clock the seas had become so violent that the ship was rolling from one beam to another. Wiping his face from the pelting rain Rogers stared out to sea at the *Dutchess* and could see that it was in trouble. 'The sail to leeward was in the water and all aback, their ship taking in a great deal of water,' he noted in his journal. 'Immediately, they loosed their spiritsail and wore her before the wind.' Expecting the crew of the *Dutchess* to stow their mainsail they would then take another reef in, 'and bring to under a two reefed mainsail and reefed and balanced mizzen,' he was surprised to see that they did not do this but kept on heading southward tossed around by the violent seas.

Ice was a major worry for Rogers and he dreaded sailing into any ice fields because of their inability to fight off the bitter cold. Firing a gun to signal the *Dutchess* to reef its mainsail and slow down Rogers did the same with the *Duke*, 'under the same reefed mainsail'. But the *Dutchess* kept going, smashed about like a cork in the violent seas. A shout came from one of his men as yet another wave crashed over their decks. Rogers, soaked, stared where the sailor was pointing and could see a white ensign in the main topmast rigging signalling that the *Dutchess* was in distress.

Despite the crashing waves plastering the decks of the *Duke* and the spray that soaked every man to the skin, they worked well, like a machine, pushing the *Duke* towards the *Dutchess*. 'We worked exceedingly well in this great sea,' Rogers later wrote in his journal. 'Just before night I was up with them again, and set our fore-sail twice reefed to keep 'em company, which I did all night.' The sea began to calm down around three the next morning, enabling the *Duke* to get closer to the *Dutchess*, and by five Rogers was within hailing distance of the *Dutchess* and asked how they fared. 'They answered they had shipped a great deal of water in lying by and the sea had broke in the cabin windows and over their stern, filling their steerage and waste.' Despite this they were otherwise all right, though everyone was very cold and wet.

The following day the weather was little better, with a raw wind bringing a cold icy rain from the north-west. Despite this, Rogers and Captain Dampier rowed across from the *Duke* to the *Dutchess* to see for themselves the damage the storm from the day before had done. 'We found 'em in a very orderly pickle,' Rogers recorded in his journal. 'Their clothes were drying, the ship and rigging covered with them from the deck to the main-top, while six more guns had been put into the hold to make the ship more lively.'

Prolonged exposure to cold and wet can bring on illness, yet so far both ships' crews were healthy. But this was not going to last long if they failed to make landfall. They had managed to get through the worst storm they had experienced so far; yet the high winds and driving rain still meant seas that few of us today could withstand in such small ships. The waves would have pounded the ships as they rose and fell on the crest of each wave, spray coming over the bows of both vessels as they fell into the trough of the next wave. Then, as they climbed up the side of the wave, their hulls would crash down as the crest of the waves broke over their hulls or rolled under them.

In that kind of sea, Rogers would climb into the *Duke*'s pinnace and be rowed across to the *Dutchess* and back to the *Duke* – remarkable considering that today communications would be by radio, satellite or video link-ups. Only the hardiest of sailors would consider leaving the comfort of today's ships to motor across to another ship in extremely rough seas to find out how that ship was faring, but in Rogers's day it was the only way he could communicate clearly.

They were now at latitude 61.53, longitude west 79.58, which Rogers says 'for ought we know is the furthest that anyone has yet been to the southward and where we have no night.' By 15 January 1709 they had navigated around Cape Horn and found themselves in the South Seas of the Pacific Ocean. Ten days after that, the *Dutchess* signalled the *Duke* that they would be in extreme difficulty if they did not find a harbour soon. Many of the men onboard were ill through lack of proper clothing and because they were almost always wet.

On the *Duke*, things were little better and Rogers knew he had to get to Juan Fernández Island as soon as he could. 'We are very uncertain of the latitude, the books laying 'em down so differently that not one chart agrees with another, and being but a small island, and in some doubts of striking it, we deisgne to hale in for the mainland to direct us.'

But by 31 January their fears were laid to rest when Rogers made Juan Fernández Island, bearing west-south-west. This began the experience that would become the famous book, *The Adventures of Robinson Crusoe*.

The following afternoon, Rogers sent their pinnace out with Captain Dover and a crew to go ashore, but as it grew dark they saw a light coming from the shore while their tender was still some distance away from the island. 'We put out lights for the boat though some were of the opinion the light we saw was our boat's,' Rogers wrote. As it got darker, though, he realized that the light was too large to be from the pinnace and so had to be coming from the shore. 'We fired one quarter deck gun and several muskets, showing lights in our shrouds that our boat might find us.' And so, by two o'clock that morning the pinnace was hoisted back aboard the *Duke*, having been towed by the *Dutchess* as the wind had increased in speed and fury. They believed the light was probably from French ships, which they would have to engage.

The following morning they tacked to the south of the island trying to get into one of its coves, but the wind was so strong it forced them back as they reefed their topsails. Coming close to the bay where they had sent the lights the night before, they expected to find their enemy; instead they found the bay clear. As the next bay and the bay after that were also clear, they concluded that the enemy had left, having caught sight of the two frigates. 'About noon, we sent our yall ashore with Captain Dover,[13] Mr Frye and six men, all armed meanwhile we and the *Dutchess* kept turning to get in.' But the wind whipping off the island kept them back, so much so that Rogers was forced to lower his topsails. 'We kept all hands to stand by our sails for fear of the winds carrying 'em away; though when the flaws were gone we had little or no wind.'

With no sign of the yall, Rogers paced the deck of the *Duke*, waiting for the boat to return. Finally, he made up his mind and ordered the pinnace with suitably armed men to be lowered into the water and sent after the first boat. 'We sent our pinnace to see what was the occasion of the yall's stay,' Rogers noted. 'We were afraid that the Spaniards had a garrison there and might have seized 'em.' But almost as soon as he had sent out the pinnace it returned with what Rogers termed an 'abundance of craw-fish and a man clothed in goat's skins who looked wilder than the first owners of them'.

This man was Alexander Selkirk, who had been left on the island for four years and four months by Captain Stradling in the ship *Cinque Ports*. Selkirk had in fact been the master of the ship when Captain Dampier had sailed in her and it was the last time that the ship had visited this island. It was Selkirk who had made the fire the night before when he'd seen the ships which he thought were English. Aboard the *Duke* Selkirk recounted his experiences to Rogers and the assembled company, which Rogers recorded in his journal. He had seen several ships pass while he was marooned on the island but only two came in to wood and water. He went to look at these two ships, but they were Spanish and as he tried to get away, they spotted him and shot at him. Had they been French ships, Selkirk told Rogers, he would have submitted, 'but chose to risk dying alone in the Island rather than fall into the hands of the Spaniards lest they murder or make a slave of him in the mine . . . the Spaniards he said had landed before he knew what they were and came so near him that he had much ado to escape.' On spotting the Spanish ships Selkirk ran into the woods with the Spanish hot on his heels, firing at him. Like a cat he climbed a tree while the Spanish stopped at the foot and shot several goats without discovering him.

As he recounted his experiences Selkirk told Rogers that he was born in the county of Fife in Scotland, in a town called Largo, and since his youth had been bred to be a sailor. When Rogers asked him why he was on the island, Selkirk answered that a difference between him and Captain Stradling had blown up and the captain had left him on the island with his clothes, bedding, a pistol, some powder, tobacco, a hatchet, a knife, a kettle, a Bible, some practical pieces and all his mathematical instruments and books – but without food. The first eight months had been the hardest. Selkirk had to battle 'the terror of being alone in such a desolate place'. To counter his melancholy he busied himself building two huts, one for sleeping in and one for 'dressing his vituals'. Both huts were built out of pimento trees and long grass and lined with the skins of the goats he had killed. He taught himself to make fire by rubbing two sticks of pimento wood together on his knees. The pimento wood burned well and acted as a fire as well as candles and gave off a very pleasant odour when it burned. Additionally, 'he employed himself in reading, singing Psalms, and praying, so that he said he was a better Christian while in this solitude than ever he was before or was afraid he should ever be again,' recounts Rogers. His books and mathematical instruments also helped him keep time and even know the days and months of the year. 'He diverted himself sometime by cutting his name on trees.'

In the first months of his abandonment, Selkirk rarely ate or slept. He would eat when he was so hungry that he had no other choice. This, according to Rogers, was partly from grief and partly from the lack of bread or salt he was used to having with his food. He never went to bed until he was so tired that he could not keep awake – always watching for passing ships to save him.

As far as fishing was concerned, Selkirk ate only crawfish, according to Rogers, which he sometimes boiled or broiled. He killed 500 goats and caught the same number, marking them on the ear and then letting them go. This was proved some thirty years later when Commodore Anson found some of Selkirk's marked goats when he landed at Juan Fernández.

Rogers says that Selkirk's way of life made him strong and a very swift runner, able to catch goats and kill them. 'He ran with wonderful swiftness through the woods and up the rocks and hills as we perceived when we employed him to catch goats for us.' He even outran the bulldog that Rogers sent with several of his fastest men to catch some of the goats. 'He tired both the dog and the men, catched the goats and brought 'em to us on his back.'

Rogers recounts an incident where Selkirk was so focused on chasing a particular goat that he caught it on the edge of a precipice that was hidden by some bushes. Both man and goat sailed over the edge and fell down the gorge pounding and rolling against the rocks. He was so bruised and dazed that he was unconscious for almost twenty-four hours before waking up and finding the dead goat under him. He could barely crawl back to his hut and was unable to leave it for ten days or so.

He soon found goat meat to be rather tasty. 'In season, he had plenty of good turnips which had been sowed there by Captain Dampier's men,'[14] Rogers recounted in his journal. As he tore through the woods chasing goats he soon wore out his shoes and his clothes. His feet became so hard that he was able to run or walk anywhere without pain. Rogers observed that it was some time after Selkirk came aboard the *Duke* that he could put shoes on again 'his feet swelled when he first came to wear 'em.'

When ships had come in to the various coves, for water and wood, quite often some of the ships' animals would get ashore. Cats and rats were his biggest problem in the early days. Rats particularly would gnaw at his feet and clothes, so he decided to start feeding the cats that had bred on the island with goat's meat and milk. The cats became so tame that they would, according to Rogers, sleep alongside Selkirk in their hundreds – and the cats took care of the rats. He even managed to tame some of the young goats, and would often sing and dance around with the kids and the cats 'so that by the care of Providence and vigour of his youth, being now about 30 years old, he came at last to conquer all the inconveniences of his solitude and to be very easy.'

When his clothes became useless to him, he made his clothes from goatskin. He also made knives from iron hoops from old rotten barrels that had been left by ships that had come in to take on water. These hoops he would beat with stones until he had some form of a blade. 'Having some linen cloth by him, he sowed himself shirts, with a nail and stitched 'em with the worsted of his old stockings, which he pulled out on purpose,' Rogers wrote. 'He had his last shirt on when we found him.'

When Selkirk first arrived on the *Duke* he could barely speak because he had not spoken in more than four years. 'We could scarce understand him for he seemed to speak his words by halves.' Selkirk then gave an account of the island itself. It must have seemed like a paradise to Rogers and his men because Selkirk said that the weather was so good that the trees and grass grow all year. There were no beasts or creatures on the island that would threaten a man's life or that were poisonous. The only largish creatures were the goats, originally put on the island to breed by Juan Fernández who had settled there along with some other Spanish families until continental Chile submitted to the Spaniards and the settlers left the island. The island itself, according to Selkirk's account of it to Rogers, was capable of maintaining a large number of people and strong enough to be easily defended.

'This of Mr Selkirk I know to be true,' Rogers wrote. 'His behaviour afterwards gave me reason to believe the account he gave me, how he spent his time, and bore up under such an affliction, in which nothing but the Divine Providence could have supported any man.'

***

On 3 February 1709, Rogers had the sails taken down and sent ashore to be mended and to make tents for the men. The sick were also transferred to the shore. Selkirk had been given the name of 'the Governour' of the island, and 'absolute monarch' by Rogers and his men. 'The Governour caught us two goats, which make excellent broth mixed with turnip tops and other greens for our sick, they being twenty in all, but not two that we account as dangerous.'

Over the next several days damage to the ships from the storms and high seas they had experienced as they sailed round the Horn was attended to. The ships were cleaned and repaired, the sails mended, water taken onboard along with other supplies from the island itself, while Selkirk continued to catch two goats a day. The island seems to have agreed with Rogers: 'It was very pleasant ashoar among the green piemento trees, which cast a refreshing smell. Our house being made by putting a sail round four of 'em and covering it a top with another so that Captain Dover and I both thought it a very agreeable seat, the weather being neither too hot nor too cold.'

However, Rogers was not there to sit under a sail and contemplate life on the island of Juan Fernández. He was there to grab as much loot as he could from French and Spanish ships and to promote British trade in the South Seas wherever he could. They had received intelligence just before leaving the Canaries that five French ships were sailing somewhere in these seas: he was itching to get going.

On 12 February 1709 the two frigates set sail from Juan Fernández, having agreed several signals between them should they become separated during a fight or in bad weather. Each of the frigates had been thoroughly cleaned and oiled so their hulls moved efficiently and swiftly through the water. Their new objective was to refresh at the islands of Lobos de la Mer. In the meantime, Rogers had modified both the pinnaces by adding a cannon in the bow of each. 'We put both pinnaces in the water to try them under sail, having fixed them each with a gun after the manner of a patterero, and all things necessary for small privateers, hoping they'll be serviceable to us in little winds to take vessels,' Rogers noted.

Through the rest of February 1709 they rapidly began running low of fresh water, vegetables and meat, so the crews of both ships were put onto three pints of water a day and other reduced rations in order to for them to remain at sea longer and not be discovered while taking on water and other supplies. By 9 March both ships were sailing along the coast of Peru some twenty miles out under a moderate south-east gale with each frigate towing their respective pinnaces. The hope was to intercept and capture some of the enemy shipping coming out of Lima. On 16 March, their luck changed: they caught sight of a sail. The *Dutchess* was closer and so quickly overtook the sail, which turned out to be a 16-ton Spanish vessel, the *Asunción*, out of Payta and bound for Cheripe with money to buy flour. Its master was Antonio Villegas, with a crew of eight Spanish Indians and another Spaniard. From the Spaniards, Rogers learned that seven French ships had sailed out of these seas six months before and that no more were to return. 'Adding that the Spaniards had such an aversion to them that at Callo, the Sea-Port for Lima, they'd killed so many French and quarrelled so frequently with 'em that none were suffered to come ashore,' Rogers wrote. He also learned that no British ships had been in the area since Captain Dampier's ship four years earlier and that Captain Stradling's ship, the *Cinque Ports*, had foundered off Barbacour with only Captain Stradling and six other men surviving. 'And being taken in their boat had been four years prisoners at Lima much worse than our Governour Selkirk whom they left on Juan Fernández.' That same morning they saw the islands of Lobos de la Mer.

There are two islands that make up Lobos de la Mer and around them are dangerous shoals. However, between them, Rogers described a 'Thorow-fair of good clear ground' and here they anchored in 20 fathoms of water. Rogers decided then to fit out the new prize as a privateer and so had her taken into a small round cove in the southernmost island. Here she was dried and her bottom well cleaned. 'She was relaunched and called the *Beginning*,' Rogers recounted. 'Captain Cooke being appointed to command her.' Rogers himself oversaw the refurbishment and relaunch of the *Beginning* as well as the building of 'a larger boat[15] for landing men, should an attempt be made upon the mainland'. The *Dutchess* offloaded her sick onto the island and was then sent to cruise around the islands and meet up with the *Beginning* once she was ready off the southernmost tip of the island.

To fit out this small bark, Rogers used a spare topmast from the *Duke*: 'This made her a new main mast, a mizzen topsail being altered to make her a mainsail,' while a new deck was built with four guns that swivelled. 'She was victualled and manned by twenty men from the *Duke* and twelve from the *Dutchess*. The *Beginning* was under the command of Mr Stratton, with each man well armed and ready for sea. She sailed out of the harbour on 20 March – a proud Captain Rogers watching her go. 'As I saw her out of the harbour with our pinnace she looks very pretty and I believe will sail well in smooth water, having all masts, sails, rigging and materials like one of the half galleys fitted out for Her Majesty's service in England.'

On 26 March another prize fell into their hands. Both the *Beginning* and the *Dutchess* captured a 50-ton Spanish vessel, the *Santa Josepha*, which was carrying a cargo of timber, cocoa, coconuts and tobacco, which Rogers had distributed amongst his men. The new prize was cleaned and renamed the *Increase*. It became the hospital ship for the little fleet where all the sick and wounded were transferred to along with a doctor from each of the two frigates. Rogers made Selkirk the master of the *Increase*. The landing boat that had been built at the same time as the *Beginning* was being refitted and launched and was put into the water to be towed behind the frigates.

To illustrate the harshness of this voyage, between 20 and 27 March 1709 three men died, one Spaniard and a Dutchman, from scurvy. Both had been put ashore and another Dutchman succumbed to the bites he had received from seals.

All was not entirely difficult for them. There were humourous incidents as well, such as the one where, as they approached Lobos, one of the officers caught sight of several birds that looked remarkably like turkeys. He was so eager to get at them, hoping for a delicious meal, that he leapt into the water from the boat without waiting for it to land. Holding his gun in one hand above his head, he waded through the surf, got to the shore and opened fire. 'But when he came to take up his game,' Rogers wrote, 'it stunk insufferably and made us merry at his mistake.'

These birds were probably a species of buzzards[16] that ate exclusively on the carcasses of dead seals, which gave off an offensive odour, as Rogers noted in his journal. 'Owing to the presence of certain unwholesome old seals, whose livers disagreed with those of our crew that eat them; the air, with the wind off shore, is loaded with an ugly noisome smell, which gave me a headache, and was complained of by all.'

Chapter 6

The Sack of Guayaquil

Information was crucial for the little fleet to survive. Much of their intelligence came from captured Spanish prisoners. For example, Rogers learned that the widow of the late Viceroy of Peru was expected to be setting sail for Mexico, the ship full of riches as well as her family, and that they would probably stop at Payta to refresh. The prisoners also said that Payta expected a French-built ship belonging to the Spaniards to soon be sailing out of Panama heavily laden and with a bishop onboard.[17] 'Payta is a common recruiting place for those who go to or from Lima,' Rogers noted, 'in their trade to Panama or to any part of the coast of Mexico.'

Acting on this advice Rogers decided to spend as much time as they could cruising unseen off Payta. On 30 March 1709 the little fleet was at sea heading for the waters around Payta. Two days later, a sail was seen on the horizon and the pinnace from the *Duke* was hoisted into the water, manned and armed with Mr Frye, the *Duke*'s first lieutenant, in command. Giving chase to the sail, the pinnace quickly caught up with the unknown ship and fired on her until the ship surrendered.

This was their first major prize, and it was a big one. Called the *Ascensión*, it was between 400 and 500 tons, 'built galleon fashion very high with galleries,' Rogers describes in his journal. Two brothers commanded this ship, Joseph and John Morell, which was bound from Panama to Lima with several passengers onboard and a cargo of dry goods and timber.

The following day, 3 April 1709, Rogers ordered the new prize to be manned, taking some of the Spaniards as prisoners while keeping the crew of ffity negroes onboard to keep the ship going. The new prize had an excellent stock of provisions, which would be a godsend for the fleet as they remained at sea. The man chosen to command the new vessel was Lieutenant Frye.

On the evening of the same day, another sail was sighted. This time the *Beginning* gave chase, overtaking her and bringing her back to the fleet in the early hours of the morning. This vessel, the *Jesus, Maria y José* was 35 tons and carried a cargo of timber from Guayaquil to Lima. Manned by eleven white men and one negro, the ship was commanded by Juan Guastellos. More men from the *Duke* and the *Dutchess* were put aboard to take charge of the captured ship. 'We agreed with the *Dutchess* and *Beginning* when and where to meet: and having all our Stations appointed, they left us,' Rogers wrote. Neither the *Ascensión* nor the *Jesus, Maria y José* were refitted or relaunched by Rogers and his officers.

Rogers was still interested in capturing the ship carrying the bishop. The new prisoners told him the bishop 'was to have come from Panama in this vessel for Lima but the Ship, the *Ascensión*, sprang a leak [at] Panama and the bishop switched to a French-built ship belonging to the Spaniards that was following them for Lima, but would stop at Payta.' They resolved to remain near Payta and wait.

At six the following evening Rogers ordered Mr Frye to take the *Ascensión* in company with the *Jesus, Maria y José* and sail off the saddle of Payta 'because the Hummocks appear in that shape with low land betwixt 'em.' He then ordered his ship to stand in for the shore but early on the morning of 5 April they spotted a ship to leeward and gave chase. He fired a signal at the ship and soon discovered it was the *Dutchess*. Rogers's sense of humour comes into play here because he kept up the chase, knowing she was his consort until the *Dutchess* had cleared for action. 'I did this to surprise them and at noon went onboard.'

The *Duke* and *Dutchess* remained together the following day and in the evening the *Beginning* came up with them. Here the commanders decided on the positions they would take up: 'The *Beginning* to keep close in with Payta, the *Dutchess* 8 leagues to leeward and I to lie right off Payta by 7 or 8 leagues.'

As the sun was setting, Rogers climbed down the side of the *Dutchess* into the waiting boat and was rowed across to the *Duke*. The following day, the *Duke* came up to the little fleet of prizes and Rogers went onboard the *Ascensión*, commanded by Mr Frye, to check that everything was all right and that he remained on station. Frye had not been idle since he had been put in command. The launch that had been built at Lobos had been fitted out with sails and oars ready to give chase to any small vessel, 'having men enough for that end in these peaceable seas,' Rogers wrote. The following day, Rogers sat down to a meal of mutton and cabbage onboard the *Ascensión* and gave Frye new instructions; then, satisfied that all was well, left him and was rowed back to the *Duke*.

That same day, 7 April 1709, a committee, called by Captain Thomas Dover, convened to decide the fate of Carleton Vanbrugh who had threatened to shoot one of the men for refusing to carry carrion-crows that Vanbrugh had shot. Vanbrugh had also verbally abused Captain Dover: so some form of punishment had to be meted out. The resolution the committee came to was for his name to be removed from the committee and his presence in any committee no longer desired. They agreed that Samuel Hopkins should take his place.

They had been at sea for some time and now had several prisoners to feed and water. The lack of water was beginning to tell and Rogers knew that they would have to go ashore to replenish and refresh soon. So, on 12 April, they held another committee to decide what to do about their provisions. They did not want to announce their presence to the Spaniards or the French, but they badly needed supplies, especially fresh water. At this meeting, held aboard the *Duke*, they decided to attack the town of Guayaquil. 'We have consulted and examined sundry pilots taken in Prizes and have several meetings on this occasion being provided with sufficient vessels to carry our men, guns, arms and other necessaries to Guayaquil,' the minutes of the meeting record.

The minutes also record that it was decided that the invasion of Guayaquil would be jointly under the command of Captain Thomas Dover, Captain Woodes Rogers and Captain Stephen Courtney, who were to land in three equal parties except for twenty-one men under the command of Captain Dampier, who were to take care of the guns and ammunition and land them in a safe place, close to the landing point so that plunder taken from the town could be easily carried back to the ships. The committee also resolved that they wholeheartedly put the success of the expedition into the hands of the commanders in the hope that their designs would remain secret 'to prevent the enemies from removing their wealth or giving us a vigorous reception.'

However, the discipline of the men could scupper the success of the invasion. The crew were a mixed bag of men from most European nations, and Rogers knew they would desert given the right opportunity; so he needed to find a way to encourage and discipline the men to follow orders. 'We know that misfortune attends sailors out of their element, and hear that they begin to murmur about the encouragements they are to expect for landing; which they alledge is a risk more than they shipped for,' Rogers wrote in his journal.

In order to induce them to put their hearts into the invasion Rogers and the committee resolved that the men would have full equal share of the plunder from the town. 'What was to be the men's share,' Rogers wrote, 'would be all manner of bedding and clothes, gold rings, buckles, buttons, liquors and provisions for our own expending and use with all sorts of arms and ammunitions, except great guns for ships is plunder and shall be divided equally between the men of each ship.'

Exempt from this booty were women's earrings with loose diamonds and precious stones, though no reason why they should be exempted is given. 'It is also agreed that any wrought silver or gold crucifixes, gold and silver watches or any other movables of any kind shall likewise be plunder.'

The rules go on to say that any of the men could go to the officers of both ships and insist on what is deemed to be plunder if he felt that more booty had been taken and not put into the store of plunder and that a committee of both ships' officers was to be immediately convened to decide if there was anything else that could be construed as plunder. At the same time, the rules stated that the owners' interests in the plunder were also to be taken into account. But if an individual stole or hid any of the plunder, especially gold, silver, precious stones, diamonds and jewels that no man already had in his possession, that would be considered a misdemeanour and the person seriously punished. Each man was to deliver the plunder he had to the appointed officer in charge and was to make sure it was done in a public way so that no one could point fingers at either the men or the officers.

The same committee also ruled that any prisoners of note should be kept as bargaining tools in case any of their men went missing. The last paragraph of the committee meeting ended in the following manner: 'To prevent all manner of mischevious ill-conduct from disorders on shore, we pressingly remind you that any officer or other than shall be so brutish as to be drunk ashore in an enemie's country, shall not only be severly punished, but lose all share of whatsovever is taken in this expedition.'

Anyone disobeying a command, running away from the action, discouraging the men to fight or acting in a cowardly way was to receive the same punishment as 'anyone who presumes to burn or destroy anything in the town without our orders, or for mischief sake, or that shall be so sneakingly barbarous as to debauch themselves with any prisoners on shore, where we have more generous things to do, both for our own benefit and the future reputation of ourselves and country.' As long as the rules were strictly followed, Rogers recorded in his journal, the hope was to surpass all other attempts of this nature and 'not only to enrich ourselves and friends, but even to gain reputation from our enemies.' This resolution was dated and signed by Captains Dover, Courtney and Rogers on 13 April 1709.

***

For the invasion of Guayaquil Rogers armed and manned two of the small prizes. But when everything was ready on 15 April they sighted another sail between them and the land. The two pinnaces were launched to go after her but in the haste of launching they forgot to mount the swivel guns.

The two small sailing vessels chased the much larger ship, catching up with her quickly as they sliced through the smooth seas. But as they approached the Spanish ship, volley after volley of partridge shot and small arms tore into their vessels as they tried to board her. Each time the pinnaces came up to the Spanish ship they were peppered with gunfire. Shot split the wood of their hulls, ripped into their sails. One man was hit and screamed from the pain of the wound. Again, they tried to bring the pinnace into boarding position and again the Spaniards fired volleys of shot at them.

Standing on the deck of the *Duke*, Rogers watched the action, wishing he was there directing operations. 'After repeated attempts to get into a position for boarding,' he wrote, 'the boats were obliged to retire much damaged, under heavy fire with the loss of two killed and three wounded.' One of those killed was his younger brother, Thomas Rogers, who 'was shot through the head and instantly died to my unspeakable sorrow but as I began this voyage with a resolution to go through it and the greatest misfortune shall not deter me, I'll as much as possible avoid being thoughtful and afflicting myself for what can't be recalled but pursue the concerns of the voyage which has hitherto allowed little respite.'

The Spanish ship was later taken that afternoon and turned out to be the *Havre de Grace*, the ship the bishop had sailed in from Panama. However, the bishop was not onboard. Ten days earlier he had landed at Point St Helena and had transferred to a different ship. Later that afternoon they added another small prize to the fleet, this one loaded with cassia soap and leather.

On 16 April they buried the dead: 'About twelve we read prayers for the dead and threw my dear brother overboard with one of our sailors, hoisting our colours half mast; and we beginning, the rest of the fleet followed, firing each some volleys of small arms.' Rogers described his younger brother as hopeful and active. His officers, he recorded, all expressed a deep regret for his loss. He was only twenty years old.

The fleet had now increased to eight vessels in addition to the two frigates, with more than 300 prisoners to feed and guard. The taking of Guayaquil was now a necessity, as fresh water and food were scarce. But in order to ensure the safety of the prisoners and that they did not escape while the invasion was under way, they were all put onto the two frigates and three of the prizes and each ship was ordered to remain at sea in formation for forty-eight hours, then they were to set sail for Point Arena and anchor there. In each of these ships, the prisoners were put in irons 'because having many more prisoners than men to guard 'em, we must have 'em well secured,' wrote Rogers.

On 17 April they made ready to go ashore. Reading out the resolution the committee had made to the men regarding plunder, Rogers received full encouragement from his men, who were eager to get going. To prevent men from losing sight of their company or getting lost, each man was given a ticket so that he knew which company he was with. Rogers also appointed the best men 'the soberest Man we could pick to command every ten men under the Captains'.

In the afternoon of 18 April everything on the frigates and the prizes was made ready for the coming invasion. All the men earmarked for the landing were put aboard the pinnaces, boats and the launch while Rogers left behind forty-two men and boys on the *Duke* under the command of Robert Frye and thirty-seven aboard the *Dutchess* under Edward Cooke's command. The prisoners were divided amongst the *Duke* and the *Dutchess* and the *Havre de Grace* guarded by heavily armed skeleton crews. In all, 201 men were set to go ashore and the rest to remain behind to guard the prisoners. However, Rogers brought seven of the most important prisoners taken from the *Havre de Grace* with him in his bark, 'fearing they might be dangerous persons to leave behind us'.

Around ten that night, they dropped anchor at Point Arena where they waited for the tide to turn. At four o'clock the following morning Rogers, in company with Captain Courtney and 'without boats and 40 men, left the barks and ordered them to lie at Puna one tide after us that we might have time to surprise Guayaquil before they should appear in sight of it to alarm them for we had notice that they keep a look-out a league below the town.'

Halfway to Puna they landed on the island at dawn – it was more of a mangrove swamp than an island, with the only hard, cleared ground around the single small settlement. Here they stayed throughout the day, hiding in their boats under a maze of mangrove branches. 'This island is not passable, being full of thick Musgroves and Swamps that swarm with moquitos.'

On 20 April, rowing and towing their small boats at night so that they could be mistaken for drift timber, they slowly and surely made their way towards the town of Puna. 'We had an excellent Indian pilot that advised us to come to Graplin about 11 at night to lie in our boats about a mile short of the town[18] and to surprise 'em at daybreak.'

Sadly, however, they lost their element of surprise. As dawn came and they drew closer to the town they were seen by an Indian who ran to the town of Puna and raised the alarm. The small Spanish garrison of twenty men ran pell mell into the woods with the townspeople, leaving only the garrison commander, Lieutenant Andres Zamora who refused to leave his post out of pride. Rogers then ordered that every boat, canoe and dugout be completely destroyed so that there would be no chance of anyone getting to Guayaquil to tell them the English had landed. By noon that day his men assured him that Puna was now cut off from the mainland. 'They took the look-outs at their posts and cut all their canoes and bark-logs to pieces and in the town.'

There were around thirty houses and a small chapel at Puna, and in the confusion Rogers managed to capture Lieutenant Zamora along with his family and twenty others. 'They assured us that there could be nobody to give notice of us to Guayaquil,' he wrote in his journal. Amongst the lieutenant's papers, Rogers found a letter that gave him some alarming news. The lieutenant had a copy of a letter that had arrived by courier from Lima addressed to Don Hieronimo Boza y Soliz, the commander and coreggidor, or mayor, of Guayaquil that had been written by the Viceroy of Peru. It stated that he was to 'keep a strict watch signifying that they had notice of Captain Dampier's coming Pilot to a squadron into these seas,' Rogers recounted. The paper had come from Lima and copies of it had been sent to all the colonies on the coast of Peru. But even more worrying was the fact that the French were the first to prepare to come out after the little English fleet. They learned of five great French ships of forty to fifty guns or more preparing to sail. Rogers, however, was optimistic. The letter was incorrect in many ways and the more Rogers studied it the more he realized that the warning had been so recently delivered to Guayaquil that the city would have had very little time to strengthen its defences. Also, the Spanish believed he had a much bigger force and his ships were much larger than they actually were so they would likely try to match that firepower by fitting out a squadron of their own ships, which would take some time. Time was on his side but not for long. Perhaps the most positive factor in his favour was that the Spanish had no idea where he was. Once he took the city of Guayaquil they would know, but as he approached he believed he still had the element of surprise. Turning to his captains he said, 'T'is certain that it is next to impossible any sufficient force can arm out from Callao the port of

Lima to be here in less than 24 days, by which time we hope to finish and be gone where they cannot find us.'

Puna had been taken in a couple of hours, but before starting the thirty-three mile trip upriver for Guayaquil he waited for the onrushing tide to come rolling in. Once it did the five little boats got under way in what Rogers described as a small rolling sea. The wind was blowing hard and it was dark as they headed for their prize. 'The boat being deep laden and cram'd with men,' Rogers wrote, 'I had rather be in a hard storm than here.'

They reached the river mouth at dawn on 21 April; by noon the little fleet was halfway towards the city. The lead boat discovered a plantation on one side of the river that they were unable to pass without being observed; so, very quietly, signals were sent from boat to boat and they had to bring their boats one by one into hiding under mangrove branches. Here they lay in their boats until darkness fell, keeping as quiet as they could. 'It was very hot and we were pester'd and stung grievously by the mosquitoes as we lay under the mangroves,' Rogers entered in his journal.

In the gloom of dusk the fleet moved out from under the mangroves back into the river and with muffled oars began to row forward, moving with stealth and secrecy past the plantation. The tide was carrying them forward, aiding their journey which Rogers felt would take six hours in reaching their target. At this point the command for the land forces would pass to Captain Dover, the captain of Marines.

On 22 April the little fleet arrived within sight of the city of Guayaquil; but it was not the sleeping city they expected to see. Indeed, on the crest of a hill close behind the city a huge beacon fire was raging, while down its slopes lanterns had also been lit. A half-mile foot bridge was outlined in the darkness by torches and went deep into the heart of the city, having been built over a marsh. Two heavy cannon were fired, their roar momentarily drowning all the shouting and crying from the townspeople. A volley of small arms was fired. Alarmed, Rogers turned to one of the Indian pilots and asked, 'What's the occasion of this? Is it a Saint's Day?' The Indian shrugged and replied, 'It is an alarm.' From the shore they heard cries that Puna had been taken. 'The enemy is coming up the river,' people shouted. At the stroke of midnight the church bells began ringing as people shouted along the shore. 'We heard a confused noise of their bells, a volley of small arms and two great guns and knew that the town was alarmed,' Rogers wrote.

This was a heaven-sent opportunity as far as Rogers was concerned. He felt that they had only just been detected, if at all, and that the town was in such confusion that there was no time to organize a defence. The time was ripe for attack. Rogers ordered his pinnace forward, heading for the shore, fully confident that the other boats would follow. However, the inexperienced and incompetent Dover panicked, sending frantic signals to all the boats to form up with him.

So, Rogers, Courtney, Dampier and Dover had a conference in the middle of the mile-wide river under darkness instead of landing and attacking as they could have done. Rogers was furious and was for going forward, landing and taking the town. They argued for hours, with Rogers demanding that the attack take place at once while the cautious Dover refused, worried that the aroused city would be too difficult to take. To Rogers's surprise Captain Courtney also erred on the side of caution. Angered, Rogers turned to Dampier and asked him what the buccaneers would have done. Dampier replied, simply: 'They never attacked a place once it was alarmed.' Now desperate, Rogers turned to his junior officers to see where they stood. 'I asked the consent of the lieutenants in all the boats about landing,' he claimed, 'telling 'em this would be the first alarm and that we had best land during the enemy's consternation but they differ'd in opinion and few were for landing.'

Rogers was now the lone voice in the wilderness and pointed out that every moment wasted arguing gave the people of the city time to hide their wealth and gather reinforcements. This changed the minds of some of the people, and indeed when Rogers called for a vote he received a small majority. But Dover was still in command and he refused, insisting that Rogers should be personally liable, financially and legally should they attack and any disasters take place.

Dover had a plan, and it was a poor one. He argued for hours against an assault as he believed their ground forces were hopelessly outnumbered. 'Dr Dover insisted on the difficulty of attempting the enemy now they had been so long alarmed saying we should but throw away our own and our men's lives,' Rogers entered in his journal. 'Dr Dover said that the town appeared large and consequently was much more able to hold out than we to attack it, that we might find the attempt very desperate.' He wanted to demand 50,000 pieces of eight from the town in return for the privateers' promise not to attack.[19]

Dover was a very cautious man. As a doctor he was a fine professional, as a military man he was ineffective. While they debated, they lost their element of surprise and what would have been a vast fortune. Rogers pointed out the flaws in the plan, the main one being why would the town pay a ransom against a force that was so small and weak they could easily defeat it? If they agreed to negotiate for the ransom they would find a way to delay and delay while all the wealth was removed from the town.

At midnight on 22 April their argument began and by two o'clock, while still arguing the tide had turned, they were forced to go back down the river three miles to a sheltered area away from the current where the argument continued for several more hours. Throughout this time they had remained hidden under the cover of darkness. From the *coreggidor*'s report of the incident the town had not been alerted. The Catholic city was, in fact, celebrating a saint's day, just as Rogers originally thought. All the lights, cannon, gunfire, torches were all part of the celebration.[20]

When the presence of the English was known Don Hieronimo hastily convened a council of war in the city. Their first action was to send couriers to the province's capital, Quito, and to the Viceroy of Peru for reinforcements. The Spaniards had no idea of the strength of the English force, so Don Hieronimo ordered that the townspeople should bury their gold, jewels and other valuables so that it was out of reach of the invaders. The gold belonging to the royal treasury of the city was secretly hidden, and by the estimate of the *coreggidor* more than £80,000 was hidden in total.

The point of putting Dover in charge of the overall expedition by the Bristol syndicate that backed the venture was because it was thought that, with his large investment, he would not overlook any chance to substantially increase his profit. Clearly, the backers were completely wrong about the man and had not taken into account his lack of military experience and his cautiousness, despite his having sailed on three expeditions before this one. It is likely that he had not had to face the decisions on those three that he now faced at Guayaquil.

The debated ended with Rogers agreeing to send two Spanish prisoners, Captain Arizabala and an English envoy under a white flag of truce to speak with the *coreggidor* for its ransom, which Rogers believed was in excess of 40,000 pieces of eight. Don Hieronimo politely listened to the offer but said that the town's coffers were empty and as he could not use the king's money to pay a ransom to English pirates, he would have to fight.

For two days the negotiations dragged on. Rogers knew the Spaniards were using the time to remove all the wealth from the city, carrying it inland. Finally, on 24 April the Spanish came back with an offer of 32,000 pieces of eight. Furious, Rogers ordered negotiations to end immediately. Talking was over; now it was time to take the city.

The boats were now lying close to the town. He ordered the interpreter to tell the Spanish '[advise] all that wished to save their lives to retire out of shot, at once hauled down our flag of truce and let fly our English field colours.' He then ordered two of the ship's big guns to be mounted onto field carriages and rolled into the launch they had built at Lobos. Captain Rogers went in the pinnace from the *Duke*, Captain Courtney in his pinnace and Captain Dover in the great launch and with seventy men altogether, some hauling the two field guns, landed on the bank of the river hauling the launch ashore. 'Mr Glendal 3rd Lieutenant of our ship tarried aboard our bark with ten men to ply our guns over our heads into the town as we landed.' The enemy pulled back up to the end of the street lining the houses on either side with snipers with muskets facing the British as they landed on the bank and headed forward. 'Fire!' ordered Rogers as each man crossed the bank, dropped to their knees and fired. Loading, they advanced while overhead cannon shot from the guns on the barks smashed into the street in front of them and into the houses. They were now too close and orders were passed back to the men on the bark to stop firing in case they hit one of their own men.

Rogers takes up the story. 'We who landed kept loading and firing very fast; but the enemy made only one discharge and retired back to their guns where their horses drew up a second time.' In the terrible heat the British advanced up a street where the enemy was lined up at the end and in houses all along the street. The British loaded and fired, advanced, loaded and fired, advanced – the air filled with the sound of shot and the smell of cordite. Reaching the first house Rogers and his men came around the side and found themselves staring down at four big guns in position in front of a large church at the end of the street. 'But as our men came in sight firing the horses scampered off.' Encouraged, Rogers shouted to his men, 'Seize the guns!' Running forward with eight or ten of his men they soon came within pistol range, 'when we all fired, some at the gunners and others at the men in arms in front of the church, where they were very numerous: but by the time we had loaded and more of our men came in sight, they began to run and quitted the guns, after firing them with round and partridge one of the last was fired to us very near but thanks be to God did us no hurt.'

The rest of the men with Captains Dover and Courtney then arrived, joining Rogers outside the church. Leaving Rogers with a few men to guard it they marched through the town taking care of any of the enemy that they encountered so that by the time they reached the other end Rogers and his landing party had taken the whole town and several prisoners along with it. 'From the time we landed till we took their guns and possession of their church I believe was not much above half an hour,' Rogers noted. Rogers joined Captain Dover at the other end of the town where there was another church and left him there with some guards, marched back into the centre of the town to another small church, which he left Captain Courtney with some men there to guard. He returned to the main church where the big guns had been posted.

Dover had a difficult night. He burned some houses that fronted the church in order flush out any enemies still there. A hill overlooked the little church where he and his men were posted and thick woods were within pistol shot of his position, 'so that the enemy were almost continuously popping at him all night,' wrote Rogers. Indeed, Dover told Rogers the next day that during the night some of the enemy appeared out of the woods but ran away as soon as a volley was fired at them. Rogers believed that had the enemy been courageous they could have taken Dover's position or indeed retaken the town itself because the British had such small numbers. 'For the town being long, we could not keep the whole without dividing at such a distance; but his firing of the houses covered the worst part of his Quarters that night which was of great service to him.'

Posting guards all around, they commandeered the Spanish guns and placed them in the large area in front of the church. Fifteen Spanish had lost their lives in the half-hour battle. Only two from the British side had been hurt, one of them mortally wounded from a cohorn shell that split when it was fired out of the cohorn mortar on one of the barks. 'We kept our colours flying on the great church and sent the Lieutenant of Puna with proposals to ransom the town,' Rogers wrote in his journal. But was it worth it? There seemed to be little in the town to match the cost of lives.

With the town secure, Rogers and his men began searching for what they came for – treasure. They searched every corner for valuables. Using axes, iron crow bars and mauls they tore open the churches, store houses and cellars in their zeal for treasure, but found nothing but flour, peas, beans and jars of wine and brandy. Rogers had great difficulty in preventing his men from tearing up 'the floor of the great church to look for treasure amongst the dead but which I would not suffer because of a contagious distemper that had swept off a number of people there not long before, so that this church floor was full of graves.'

Carrying what little plunder there was down to the waterside soon took its toll. The weather was so hot and humid that carrying these large jars of the wine, brandy and other spirits down to the waterline was too much for his exhausted men to handle.

In the 'great church' Rogers found a gold-headed cane and another with a silver head which, he remarks, would have been carried by chief officers, none under the rank of captain, so that those men who had carried them, he surmised, must have been in some haste to leave. 'Besides carrying off these badges of office we unhung a small church bell and sent it aboard for our ships use,' he explained.

In all this did not amount to much. However, one of the Indians whom Rogers had personally taken prisoner told him there was money up the river. To investigate this claim, Rogers and Courtney decided to dispatch twenty-one men under the command of Lieutenant Connelly to take the pinnace from the *Dutchess* and go up the river. At this point Rogers wanted to send both pinnaces up the river to seize the wealth as it would save them time, but everyone else was against this plan, anxious that if the enemy attacked the next morning they would not have enough men to counter the attack.

The men found houses mostly filled with women, especially at one house 'where there were above a dozen handsome genteel young women, well dressed and their hair tied with ribbons very neatly, from whom the men got several gold chains, but were otherwise so civil to them that the ladies offered to dress 'em victual and brought 'em a cask of good liquor.' Rogers goes on to say that 'I mention as a proof of our sailors modesty and out of respect to Mr Connelly and Mr Selkirk, the late Governor of Juan Fernández who commanded this party: for being young men, I was willing to do 'em this justice, hoping the fair sex will make 'em a greatful return when we arrive in Great Britain on account of their civil behaviour to these charming prisoners.'

The party of twenty-one men brought back with them gold chains and plates to the value of more than £1,000. But they also came with some alarming news, having seen in some places above the little village where the women had been, more than 300 armed infantry. 'The enemy design to gain time by pretending to pay ransom till, with vast odds they may attack us and reckon themselves sure of victory,' Rogers wrote in his journal. Indeed, the last entry for 24 April talks about how tired he was: 'The fatigue I have had since I left our ships in this hot weather has weakened and disordered me very much.'

By 26 April the Spanish came back with an offer of 30,000 pieces of eight for the ransom for the town, its ships and barks, to be paid in twelve days. Rogers found this derisory and sent back a reply to the effect that he would burn the town by three that afternoon unless they agreed to give sufficient hostages for the money to be paid in six days rather than twelve. At two that afternoon the prisoners who had been taking the messages between the two sides returned with two men on horseback as hostages with a verbal agreement from the Spanish. The signed agreement arrived the following morning. An English one was sent in return.

Both hostages also signed the agreement so that by 26 April at eleven o'clock the British marched out of Guayaquil with Rogers in the rear: 'we made what show and noise we could with our drums, trumpets, our colours flying and our guns and thus took leave of the Spaniards very cheerfully. I marching in the rear with a few men picked up several pistols, poleaxes, cutlashes which shew'd that our men were grown very careless, weak and weary of being soldiers and that t'was time to be gone from hence.'

Was the invasion worth it? In his journal Rogers states he was pleased to be leaving Guayaquil with the deal that they had made but not half as pleased as he would have been if they had been able to take the town by surprise. He had been assured by all his men that there should have been upwards of 200,000 pieces of eight in money in the town and greater stores than they now had. These included 250 bags of flour, beans and peas, and rice, fifteen jars of oil, about 160 jars of other liquors, some cordage, ironware and small nails, with four jars of powder, a ton of pitch and tar, a parcel of clothing and necessaries, about £1,200 in plate, earrings, and 150 bales of dry goods, four guns and 200 useless Spanish arms and musket barrels, a few packs of indigo, cocoa, and about a ton of loaf sugar. 'Besides these which we took, . . . we left abundance of goods in the town, with liquors of most sorts, sea stores several warehouses full of cocoa, divers ships on the stocks, and two new ships unrigged upwards of 400 tons, which cost 80,000 crowns and lay at anchor before the town.'

But he believed that a ransom for the things left behind was far better than for them to burn what they were unable to carry. Presumably, he was thinking of the relations between Great Britain and Spain and the reputation that these English privateers were not pirates, butchers or vandals. We must also assume he was thinking of the French ships being fitted out and ready to sail to intercept them. The longer they waited to burn and pillage in the city the more chance they had of being captured.

Friendly fire was just as much a problem for Rogers as it is today. For example, 'a French man belonging to my company, sent with others to strengthen Captain Courtney's quarters, being put centinel shot Hugh Tidcomb one of our men so that he died,' Rogers explained in his journal. The reason for this, he felt, was the result of an order that was too severe, stating that any man would be shot in the night who did not answer. 'Neither this man nor the centinel understood how to ask or answer the watchword. By which neglect a man was unaccountably lost.'

During the confusion of a night attack another man was shot in the middle of his poleaxe which was hung at his side.[21] The ball smashed into the iron and bruised the man but did not hurt him, 'so it proved to be a piece of armour well placed,' Rogers wrote.

Another accident occurred as one of Captain Courtney's men was wounded when the pistol he was carrying at his side accidentally went off, lodging a pistol ball in the thickest part of his leg. Only one man broke the rules – a Dutchman who got so drunk on brandy and wine that he was missing for two days and only roused out of his stupor and brought onboard when they were ready to sail.

Rogers was not a cruel man by any means and he treated all his prisoners with civility and respect. This he shows in one of his entries after the battle of Guayaquil, as they were about to set sail. 'On parting with the Lieutenant of Puna I gave him 4 old sick negroes and a damaged bail of goods for what we had taken from him, being a man we had some respect for; and that I also parted very friendly with several of our prisoners we took at sea, particularly an old padre that I had treated civilly at my own table ever since we took him, for which he was extremely thankful.'

Rogers equated their expedition and taking of the town with what the French had done twenty-two years previously. The French buccaneers whom Rogers referred to as pirates 'left their infamous mark when in their attack on the place they lost a great many men and afterwards committed a great deal of brutishness and murder.' But apart from brutishness and murder Rogers was no more than a pirate himself. He had plundered a town not for any strategic or military value but for wealth. He thought of himself as above pirates and considered the tales of their exploits to be fabrications or exaggerated and of no value to future navigators.

By the end of April they had left Guayaquil and were sailing down the river towards Puna, where they picked up the ships and men they had left behind. These men were very glad to see Rogers, Courtney and Dover and were anxious to hear about the plunder of the town. At the same time, Rogers had the plunder moved from the barks into the large galleon, the *Havre de Grace*.

On 30 April another prize was taken. Seeing a sail running up the channel towards Guayaquil the boat from the *Havre de Grace* was sent in pursuit but the pinnace from the *Duke* being faster it was sent off and took the enemy vessel at sunset. It was a Spanish bark of more than 30 tons coming from Sania.

It had a crew of seven including the ship's master, and was filled with bags of flour, beans, peas, 200 sugar loaves, several frails of quinces, sugarplums and other sweetmeats along with large quantities of pomegranates, apples and onions with some dried beef and country cheese. The ship had been out for seven days and had not heard about the taking of Puna and Guayaquil but had learned of the warning given to the Lieutenant General of Puna about a British squadron being in these waters.

As the month of May began the hostages were becoming more and more uneasy, wondering if the ransom was going to be paid for them. The deadline was fast approaching and finally, on the last day of the agreed ransom demand, the Spanish sent a boat to meet the British bringing with them 22,000 pieces of eight as part of the ransom. Rogers did not release the hostages, telling the Spaniards that the rest must come before the hostages could go.

Tides and waiting for the ransom delayed their departure from Puna. 'About a league before the town of Puna I saw the *Havre de Grace* at anchore near the edge of a shoal,' Rogers wrote in his journal. The pinnace from the *Dutchess* with Captains Courtney, Dover and Dampier were coming away from the large galleon to Rogers, apparently in trouble. Leaving them on the *Duke*, Rogers went aboard the *Havre de Grace* on the afternoon of 5 May and 'got her out of danger and into the Channel but came to anchor on the advice of Senior Morell and the Indian pilot.' But as there was no wind, he could not get the *Havre de Grace* sailing again and had to come to anchor near a shoal where they waited for twenty-four hours before the wind came up.

During this time the hostages became more and more agitated. 'It's worse than death they say to be carried to Great Britain,' Rogers wrote in his journal. The time was well past the final payment day. As he got everyone onboard and ready to sail they waited for the Spaniards to come for them with the rest of the ransom. It was not until 7 May that a Spanish boat arrived at Point Arena and would go no further. They climbed aboard one of the four barks that Rogers had left as agreed and brought an additional 3,500 pieces of eight.

On the following day most of the prisoners were released. 'We discharged all our prisoners except the Morells, a little Dutchman and a Gentleman's Son from Panama,' Rogers entered in his journal. 'Along with our Indian pilots that I took aboard to amuse the people of Guayaquil that we should return thither and 2 more that desired to stay with us besides the 3 Ransomers.' The gentleman's son had gold chains and what Rogers refers to as 'other moveables', which he used to purchase the *Beginning* from the English. They parted as good friends in good company with some of the prisoners telling them more Spaniards were interested in trading with them and would meet them later on. But Rogers and his officers were for sailing as soon as they could. They knew the French had large ships that by now must have been at sea looking for them. His officers wanted to get away and head for the Galapagos Islands. And so, around 11 May, they set sail and left Puna for good.

But more trouble faced him as they sailed away from Guayaquil. On 11 May 1709 seventy men in both the *Duke* and *Dutchess* became sick with fever. These were mostly men who had taken part on the attack on Guayaquil, and so it was surmised that this was where they had contracted the fever. Captain Courtney was one of those who succumbed and Captain Dover went onboard to treat him. A few days later, Mr Hopkins, Dover's assistant and his kinsman, died of the fever.

As they headed for the Galapagos Islands a day hardly went by when Rogers did not write about another death in his journal. Sixty men onboard the *Duke* were sick, and eighty onboard the *Dutchess*. Though they had enough doctors their medical supplies were fast running out. Rogers needed fresh water quickly, but to preserve the health of those who had not succumbed to the fever Rogers prescribed punch: 'Finding punch may preserve my own health I did at this time prescribe it freely among such of our company as were well to preserve theirs.'

Reaching the Galapagos Islands they searched each one for fresh water and found very little, not enough for everyone onboard their little fleet. Knowing the levels of fresh water, medicines and stores were reaching a critical level Rogers had no choice but to steer a course for the island of Gorgona.

Chapter 7

Battles at Sea

As they cruised amongst the Galapagos Islands searching for fresh water they took two more small prizes but one of the recent prizes, a small bark under the command of Mr Hartley, was feared lost with only two days' water supply. The supposition was that the three-man crew had been overpowered during the night by the two Spaniards and three negro prisoners they had onboard. Time was short and so was their supply of fresh water. The loss of Hartley meant that for some time they had to search for him and his bark as well as for fresh water amongst the vastness of the Galapagos archipelago, which stretches nearly 3,000 miles and is made up of thirteen large and more than 200 smaller islands. To find water would be like finding a needle in a haystack!

In fact, Rogers later learned when he returned to England that after staying at sea for a fortnight without water Hartley was finally forced to head for the mainland where he and the crew were captured by Spanish Indians, tied to a tree, whipped and beaten. He was only saved by a padre who ordered the men to be cut down. He then spent some time in Lima before returning to England.

Nine days of searching for water and Hartley proved futile. They did however capture hundreds of turtles for meat. They had water enough for a journey to the tropical island of Gorgona just off Colombia, where Rogers knew he could get fresh water. Gorgona was a rain-swept island and would provide his sick and dying with the fresh water and food they so desperately needed. So he gave up the search and set sail for Gorgona.

Gorgona was not in Rogers's plans. All along he had planned to attack the treasure galleons that sailed out of Manila to Acapulco in Mexico. His main aim at this stage was to intercept the Manila galleon that the Spanish had told them about as well as raiding ports and settlements along the way. Also, he knew that in that part of Mexico the Spanish had no large fleets, so he would be relatively safe once in Mexican waters.

But he had to go to Gorgona. If he did not he would have to abandon the expedition because he did not have enough healthy men to handle the ships in the squadron[22] and there were none to man the guns. He had no choice.

Within hours of dropping anchor at Gorgona the pinnaces of both the *Duke* and the *Dutchess* took the second of the two barks they captured here. The first was entirely worthless and the second appeared to be the same, but after a quick search of her holds they discovered bags of gold dust, the payment to the crew for the cargo they had delivered at their last port. This bark, commanded by Captain Enriques, was on its way back to its home port of Guayaquil.

When this gold was discovered, Rogers was laid low with dysentery. Enriques was questioned by Captain Dover and Captain Courtney. They wanted to know where his gold had come from: he told them it came from Colombian gold mines at San Juan, several days' rowing up a shallow river that emptied out into the Pacific sixty miles south-east of Gorgona.

Dover and Courtney, now both gripped by greed, hatched a ridiculous plan to take the squadron to the mouth of the river, anchor it there, row upstream and raid the mines. The problem was the sick and dying. They had only just arrived at the island and nothing had been done to get the sick off the boats and onto the beaches under tents. Nothing had been done to bring in fresh water.

Dover and Courtney completely ignored this fact and hastily convened a committee on the *Dutchess*, out of Rogers's earshot. The committee unanimously agreed the plot without thinking about the consequences. When Rogers heard about it the following morning he was furious and called in the Morell brothers who had commanded the *Ascensión* and Juan Navarro who commanded the other bark they took at Gorgona.

They told him that there was no safe anchorage at the mouth of the river and that their ships would probably end up aground. Also, the river itself had heavily wooded banks and in places was so narrow that a tree cut down and laid across the narrowest points would bridge the river. Indeed, the local Indians were loyal to the Spanish and could easily cut down trees in front and behind the English boats as they made their way up the river, leaving them with nowhere to go. They would then have no problem in massacring the English at their leisure with their poisoned arrows.

Rogers treated his prisoners with courtesy and civility at all times and it may have been because of this that they were more inclined to tell him things that they may not have told others. 'I was surprised that the committee had not inform'd themselves somewhat better before they resolv'd on going to this place, and immediately sent to undeceive our officers,' Rogers wrote.

Dover, meanwhile, was not happy. Not only had Rogers pointed out the utter stupidity of the plan, there was also the fact that he had probably saved Dover from a terrible fate, something the bull-headed doctor refused to see as positive. Instead, whenever anyone was in earshot he would openly show his dislike of Rogers, questioning his handling of the voyage. 'We have lately had almost a general misunderstanding amongst our chief Officers, and some great abuses which I suppose sprung at first from several unhappy differences arising at and before our attempt on Guayaquil,' Rogers observed in his journal.

There were more pressing things to be done. Even suffering from dysentery Rogers supervised the offloading of the sick and dying men and the erection of as many tents as they could set up from the sails from their ships. Indeed, they soon had a tent city onshore, which they named Little Bristol. The worst of the sick could not be moved for weeks and lay in the hospital tents as they slowly recovered. Some, however, were too far gone, and died. But for those who were healthy the stay on Gorgona was not a holiday: the *Duke* and the *Dutchess* had to be cleaned, scraped and refitted.

The *Havre de Grace* also badly needed a refit as her yard-arms were cracked and the sails were riddled with mildew, while the rudder and a large part of the bow were full of woodworm and the ropes, rigging and lines were unusable. So the refitting of the *Havre de Grace* took much longer than they expected. By mid-July most of these defects had been repaired and her own twelve guns were mounted along with two each from the *Duke* and the *Dutchess* and the four field guns they had captured at Guayaquil, giving her a complement of twenty guns. They renamed her the *Marquis* and, according to Rogers, 'the ship looked well so that we all rejoic'd in our new consort to cruise with us.' Looks, however, would prove deceptive; the *Marquis* would turn out to be a poor sailing vessel.

While rummaging through her cargo in order to clean her they found 500 bales of Spanish religious documents, which took up a huge amount of room in the ship. These they threw overboard with the exception of those they used to burn the pitch off their ships' bottoms. At this point in his journal Rogers tells of the superstitions of the Roman Catholic prisoners. His own feelings towards the pope and the stories about miracles he takes very lightly, always looking to have a shot at the pope. 'The stories I heard I took 'em to have been invented merely to ridicule the Romanists; but when I found such silly stories believed by eight grave men of a handsome appearance and good reputation amongst the Spaniards, I was convinced of the ignorance and credulity of the Papists.'

The incident that brought this about was that, while getting rid of the cargo from the *Marquis* in order to clean her, a large wooden effigy of the Virgin Mary was either dropped or thrown overboard and carried ashore by the currents to the northern part of the island. Here some Indians who were fishing pulled it out of the water and put it in their canoes, bringing it to the shore 'over against our ship where we gave our prisoners liberty to walk that day'.

These prisoners, Rogers wrote in his journal, immediately crossed and blessed themselves when they saw the effigy thinking it had come from Lima to help them. 'They set the image up on shore and wiped it dry with cotton and when they came aboard told us, that though they'd wiped her again and again, she continued to sweat very much,' Rogers wrote. 'All those around were devoutly amazed, praying and telling their beads. They showed this cotton to the ransomers and the interpreter wet by the excessive sweat of the Holy Virgin, which they kept as a choice relick.'

Rogers was by no means a bigot when it came to the Catholic faith. He was, if anything, a bigot of social class, for in his treatment of those of the higher classes he wrote in his journal that 'we allowed liberty of conscience onboard our floating commonwealth, and there being a priest in each ship, they had the great cabin for their mess whilst we used the Church of England service over them on the quarter deck; so that the papists here were the Low Church men.'

Rogers had other things to think about as well. The taking of Guayaquil by some members of this 'floating commonwealth' was seen as a failure: some thought the plunder they gained from the action had gone to the officers and not to the sailors. Sixty men on the *Duke* signed a petition to this effect. Rogers's response was firm. He put the ringleaders into the bilboes while also cutting down the share of three of the officers, those presumably who had received more than they should. But of his crew Rogers said: 'sailors usually exceed all measures when left to themselves on these occasions and I must own that ours have been more obedient than any ships crew engaged in a like undertaking that I ever heard of.'

It must be remembered at this juncture that he had a small ship with half his crew sick and a fleet of prizes both big and small that were also full of sick men and prisoners who had to be guarded. He could have cut the prizes loose or put all the prisoners on one or two of the ships and let them go; but he didn't. Instead, he had to deal with all these different personalities. Though at the time it must have been galling for him, given his wish to sail and plunder, the experience stood him in good stead for his first stint as Governor of the Bahamas. 'If any sea officer thinks himself endowed with patience and industry, let him command a privateer and discharge his office well in a distant voyage,' Rogers growled in his journal. 'I'll engage he shall not want opportunities to improve, if not to exchange all his stock.'

To illustrate some of the difficulties he faced, most notably accommodation, we need to look at the prisoners taken aboard the *Havre de Grace*, on which the bishop had lately sailed. Amongst the prisoners on this vessel was a gentlewoman and her family. 'Her eldest daughter, a pretty young woman of about 18 newly married and her husband with her, to whom we assigned the great cabin of the prize none were suffered to intrude amongst them,' Rogers wrote in his journal. However, the young husband was a jealous man and Rogers describes jealousy as a 'Spanish epidemic' and continued with 'I hope he had not the least reason for it amongst us, my third lieutenant, Glendall, alone having charge of the ship, who being above 50 years of age appeared to us the most secure guardian to females that had the least charm.'

On top of the problems of housing men and women, some married, some not, he also had animals in abundance on the ship. One such was a creature that Rogers considered ugly and which the Spaniards called a sloth. 'Being let go at the lower part of the mizzen shrouds was two hours getting to the masthead, keeping all the time an equal and slow pace as if he walked by art and all his movements had been directed by clockwork within him,' Rogers recorded.

On the island of Gorgona they shot many monkeys, which Captain Dampier considered to be delicacies but which the officers of the *Duke* would not approach. Also onboard were the tortoises from the Galapagos Islands, which Rogers considered to be the ugliest creatures on earth. He describes them as having jet black shells like the top of a hackney coach, with a long neck about as thick as a man's wrist, club feet as big as a man's fist shaped like the feet of elephants with a little head and face that resembled a snake, so that the overall impression was very odd, old and black. 'They lay eggs on our deck about the size of gooses white with a large thick shell exactly round.'

Throughout their stay at the island of Gorgona Alexander Selkirk, commanding the *Increase*, was ferrying the Morell brothers and Captain Navarro back and forth to a Spanish settlement on the mainland. The reason for these trips was to sell off the surplus plunder they had picked up but could not get onto their fighting ships. It was on these trips that Selkirk found merchants interested in buying surplus goods. He also managed to find a Spanish merchant with enough gold to buy the *Increase*.

Captain Navarro and the Morell brothers were able to raise enough money to buy their ships back[23], and it was during these many trips to the mainland that the Morells repaid the kindness Rogers had shown them by telling him that the entire Colombian coast had been alerted to the presence of the English privateers and most men were armed. Rogers knew it was time to go.

In gratitude for their information Rogers gave the Morells everything that they couldn't take with them, and on 7 August they left Gorgona, saying farewell to their tent city, Little Bristol, and headed out to sea. For two and half months they had been at Gorgona, which had fresh water but very little in the way of vegetables and meat, so their provisions were still low. Rogers now had to make for a place where he could get these supplies, the village of Tecames on the mainland. Captain Dampier had been there many years before and remembered it as a place full of fresh food. On 25 August they raised their anchors and left the island of Gorgona, heading towards Tecames, where Rogers hoped to trade with the Indians and the Spanish for fresh provisions.

The natives here were at first ready to fight the British as they brought their ships onto the beach for careening. While the hulls and bottoms of each ship were cleaned and repaired Rogers ensured that half the men were armed and stood guard, until he came up with an idea that eased their tension. Onboard the *Duke* he had three large wooden Spanish saints, which he gave to the Spanish Indians along with a feathered cap for the chief's wife. This stopped the attacks by the Indians and made things much calmer for them.

Realizing that he needed as many men as he could use with so many sick, Rogers turned to some of the healthy negroes he had aboard the *Duke* and gathered up thirty-five of them. These men were slaves and, as he could not sell them at this time, he decided to do something else with them. Mustering them in a line on the beach, a sea breeze gently moving the trees, Rogers looked at them and began to take down the names of those who had names and named those who did not. Standing with him was Michael Kendall, a free black man from Jamaica who had escaped from his Spanish masters. Rogers turned to Kendall. 'You are to drill these men continually, Mr Kendall, to act as marines in case we meet an enemy.' The men were then given arms and powder and placed in Kendall's charge. But before the drilling began Rogers gave the men baize, a rough wool or cotton, for them to wear to make them look more respectable, and a dram of rum. Then he turned to them: 'You must now look upon yourselves as Englishmen and no more as slaves to the Spaniards,' he said.

In that far flung place, Rogers did what the British parliament did not do until decades later, which was to free the slaves under him. True, he needed them to act as a company of marines, but, nevertheless, he had freed slaves well before it became fashionable. 'They expressed themselves highly pleased,' Rogers wrote, 'while I promise myself good assistance from them, bearing in mind the proverb, that those who know nothing of danger, fear none.'

On one occasion they decided to test the fighting efficiency of the men when the *Dutchess* raised Spanish colours. Immediately the mock fight was on. Rogers barked orders as he walked the deck of the *Duke*, while all around him his men worked to get extra speed from the *Duke* and get her within firing range of the *Dutchess*, which they did. 'During which everyone acted the part he ought have done if in earnest, firing with ball excepted,' Rogers recorded in his journal. Sails flapped in the wind as the two ships went through their mock battle. Gun crews manned their stations, following the orders shouted out by the gun captains. Cannon were primed, ready to fire, but did not fire. The prisoners had been secured in the hold along with the ships' surgeons. Red lead had been mixed with water and was thrown on some of the men to mimic blood, making the exercise as real as possible. The men covered in the mixture were sent below to the surgeons 'who were much surprised and thinking they had been really wounded went about to dress them, but finding their mistake, it was a very agreeable diversion.'

Rogers adds a footnote to this incident by talking about a Welshman who thought they were about to engage the *Dutchess* until he saw the Spanish colours the ship was flying and was so enthusiastic at the prospect of capturing a great prize he loaded his musket with real shot against all orders and was ready to fire at the crew of the *Dutchess*, 'which he would certainly have done had he not been forbid. By which it appears the blundering fool may have courage.'

Aboard the *Duke* a committee meeting had been called to pass measures against those men caught gambling, an activity that had expanded during this period of inactivity between the officers and men. Many had lost most of their share of the plunder. One measure passed at this time was a most useful one that rejected all debts between each man unless it was witnessed and attested by the commanders and put on the ship's books. This resolution was 'agreed to and signed by the officers and men in each ship in sight of California Nov, 11th 1709.'

This tedious part of the voyage was interrupted only a few times when they first anchored at the island of Tres Marias for wood, water and other supplies. They also returned to the Galapagos Islands in search of Hartley and his men, trying to discover what happened to him, but all they found was the wreckage of a boat and broken wine jars.

At this time an important event took place onboard the *Duke* when an Indian girl gave birth. The girl was from Guayaquil, among those brought aboard to act as laundresses and seamstresses on the ships. This was not uncommon in those days. In Nelson's time and later women, sometimes wives of petty officers, were onboard ships to wash and sew and help the surgeons during action. The mother and baby were well taken care of and she was given a little privacy along with a bottle of strong Peruvian wine.

Provisions were also running low. At Tres Marias they captured turtles for meat but hundreds died and had to be thrown overboard. The other turtles caught at the Galapagos had already been consumed. Though they had stopped to take on wood and water, provisions like vegetables, meat and bread were extremely scarce. Meanwhile, Rogers had the Manila ships on his his mind.

The Spanish galleons that sailed out of Manila bringing riches from the East to Acapulco, where they were shipped overland and sent by galleon across the Atlantic to Spain and the rest of Europe, were considered to be the greatest prizes sailing the seas. They were always loaded with treasure and so had to be well armed, in some cases they were floating fortresses. Built in Manila from strong hard tropical wood, these galleons were very difficult to capture or destroy, as Rogers would soon find out, their hulls being so thick that they were almost impervious to cannon balls.[24] So any commander who could capture one of these Spanish treasure ships intact was truly realizing a sailor's dream.

For 250 years, from 1565 to 1815, these massive ships, some more than 2,000 tons, plied the Pacific Ocean out of Manila to the bay at Acapulco. They carried riches in both directions. To those in New Spain (Mexico, Central America and California) Peru and other Spanish colonies they brought treasures from the East, while to the people of the Orient they brought silver pesos. Great cargo ships from eastern countries such as Japan, China and India sailed to Manila to sell their goods there, and when that merchandise arrived at Acapulco it was then sold on to those wealthy Spaniards along the Mexican and Peruvian coastal towns and cities, or sent overland to be shipped to Madrid.

These galleons carried some of the finest things money could buy at the time. Most sought-after in the European markets were spices and silks, so scarce in the Old World that people were prepared to pay large sums for them. But other riches such as rubies, pearls, jade, gold and silver plate and so much more were also carried on these galleons.

Weather was the driving factor when it came to the departure of these ships from Manila to Mexico, and their route was a circuitous one. Working free of headwinds once away from Guam they would enter the North Pacific eastward current, which would take them so far to the north that they often felt the cold icy winds coming down from the Bering Strait. From Hawaii to the Aleutians the galleons would have to ply those seas until making their first landfall at Cape Mendocino in northern California. From there the route to Mexico took them down the coast of California to Cape San Lucas and from there to Acapulco.

Rogers knew from several books in his cabin, written by other adventurers and privateers who had either travelled on these galleons or who knew these waters, that the galleons would reach Cape San Lucas in November.[25] He had planned to have his fleet cruising off San Lucas by November in order to lay a trap for one of them. The English fleet arrived on 3 November and on the afternoon of the 24th Rogers climbed aboard the yawl from the *Duke* and was rowed across to the *Dutchess* accompanied by Lieutenant Glendall, where a short conference was convened between the captains and the officers. They agreed on what landmarks they should be looking for and on the landmarks that would enable them to know their positions. 'We then agreed that the *Marquis* should now be in the middle with the *Dutchess* next the shore,' Rogers wrote. Two days later, Captain Courtney and Rogers agreed that the ship closest to the shore should switch every two days with the ship furthest out which would give them a better chance Rogers says of seeing the Manila ship. Rogers ordered his ships to sail in a line west of the Cape, with the *Dutchess* cruising only fifteen miles out, while the *Marquis* cruised in the middle and the *Duke* sailed forty-five miles from shore on the far end of the line. Selkirk shuttled between these ships on one of the smaller captured prizes, the *Jesus, Maria y José*, to take communications and supplies.

The ships were set to attention stations. Anything that could move or slide during a battle, or that would send splinters flying in all directions from a cannon ball, was secured below decks. The gun decks were cleaned and painted blood-red. Two days later the squadron was ready for action.

But there was no sight of the Manila ship. Each day they cruised the coast waiting and looking for their prize, provisions dwindled. Men were on rations and those superstitious amongst them blamed a skull they had seen at Tres Marias. Days went by, then weeks. By mid-November there was still no sign of the Manila ship.

Things were going wrong everywhere. On 22 November the *Duke* sprang a leak that forced them to set up a pump that was continuously kept going by men working in shifts. The next day the main gallantmast broke, and while trying to hoist a new one in place the rope broke and the new gallantmast came crashing down to the deck. Lucikily, no one was hurt, but the crew thought it a bad omen. On 24 November Captain Courtney discovered that the ship's meagre fresh water supplies were missing. He sent his pinnace into Puerto Seguro, lower California for more, and they only managed to come back with three barrels. Four days later the main yard-arm on the *Duke* broke free of the worn and frayed ropes and crashed to the deck. Again, no one was hurt. But each incident was a sign that things were not right. That night, two very hungry men broke into the food locker on the *Duke* and stole some bread. Rogers had all them whipped and put in irons.

As the days went by and December came, Rogers grew increasingly worried. He was acutely aware of their lack of supplies and food. Asking his men to fight a large, more powerful foe on empty bellies could be a recipe for disaster. But to leave the trap now to search for food would mean losing the opportunity of such a big prize.

On 9 December there was some small relief from the lack of provisions when the local Indians from San Lucas gave the men aboard the *Duke* a gift of dolphins, which they promptly feasted on. Rogers was glum. 'We are now something dubious of seeing the Manila ship,' he wrote. 'It's nearly a month after the time they generally fall in with this coast.'

They had food for only seventy more days. Rogers could not backtrack to Cape Horn because the Spanish would be searching for him in those waters. The only way he could go was towards Guam, which was more than 6,000 miles away. Writing in his journal, Rogers calculated that if they had favourable winds they might make it in fifty days, without taking account of storms. He needed nine days in Puerto Seguro to overhaul the ships for the long voyage and bring on wood and water. A single storm could easily erase their very small margin of safety.

A search through all the ships was conducted to see what the state of their provisions really was. Around the same time, the *Marquis* was leaking and needed to be repaired. It was taken to Puerto Seguro Bay, now the harbour town of San Lucas, for the repairs to be carried out there. At the same time, Rogers ordered the *Marquis* to be re-rigged in order to make her sail a little better.

Rogers called a committee meeting and laid the facts before the members. The lack of provisions, their very tight margin of safety if they acted now and went into Puerto Seguro to overhaul the ships, what would happen if they ran into a storm that blew them off course, concluding with the facts that they had to make for Guam as soon as they could and abandon the search for the Manila ship. The committee agreed. 'So that we all looked very melancholy, necessity compelling us to no longer continue cruising for the Manila ship, but sail at once across the Pacific for the island of Guam in order to revictual before starting for China and the Indies, and then round the Cape of Good Hope for

England,' Rogers entered into his journal.

This disappointment was short-lived: after being marooned on a calm glassy sea with no wind the night before as they were heading into Puerto Seguro, on 21 December at nine o'clock in the morning the lookout in the *Duke* 'at the mast head cry'd out he saw another sail bearing west half south of us, distant about 7 leagues [twenty-one miles]. We immediately hoisted our ensign and bore away after her but it falling calm again I ordered the pinnace to be manned and armed and sent away after her.'

At first Rogers and his officers believed it was the *Marquis* returning to the fleet. The pinnace could not get close enough even with the men rowing to properly identify the ship because the sea was so calm. 'So I sent Mr Frye in our yawl to know what news,' Rogers entered in his journal. The longboat had to row for hours getting closer to the unknown sail and when they came back several hours later they had good news. 'It was the ship we had so patiently waited for and despaired of ever seeing,' which, says Rogers, 'kept them all in a very uncertain languishing condition and the chase had to be tended during the night by two pinnaces showing false fires, that we might know the whereabouts they and the chase was.'

Despite the calm sea, the chase was on. Sand was thrown across the decks to stop them from becoming slippery with blood. The men set up nets under the masts in the event that rigging might come tumbling down, shot off by cannon fire. To stop flying splinters hammocks and bedding were stuffed in their netting while sheets of lead and wads of oakum were laid out to plug leaks from small arms fire and cannon shot at the waterline. To prevent the men from scuttling to safety while the fight was on, hatches were shut tight.

Surgeons lit their lanterns below decks, spreading canvas on the wooden operating tables and laying out their instruments, knives, saws, probes, ligatures and gags to stop the men from screaming as they cut off arms or legs while assistants brought boiling pitch that the surgeons used to cauterize the men's wounds.

On the gun decks preparations for battle were under way. In the cramped space, the sweating gunners used the tackle to push the guns forward so their muzzles were as far outboard of the ship's side as possible to avoid the fire that belched from their muzzles with every shot catching the wooden sides of the hull and setting their own ship on fire. For ammunition, round shot was placed onto the ready racks for the gunners to ram into the barrels of the cannons to pound the enemy's hull. The gunners also filled cans with iron bits and rusty metal designed to cut men down with flying shrapnel. These were also placed on the ready racks.

The gun captains too made themselves ready, filling one tub with salt to put out fires, and for cooling down red-hot gun barrels, filling another tub with vinegar water. For lighting the powder trains that ran from the gun touch-holes to ignite the explosive cartridge behind the shot the gun captains made ready their matches, made of cotton rope, which were boiled in a lead solution that made them hard and slow burning.

Far below the waterline in the magazines the men toiled quickly, sweating profusely in the heat, making up extra cartridges by filling flannel bags from the kegs of gunpowder. Wet blankets were nailed over doorways and any other openings to avoid sparks flying into the magazines and igniting the powder. Each blanket had a small hole cut out of it for the men to pass the ammunition bags to the 'powder monkeys' who waited on the other side. The 'powder monkeys' were the men who would carry the explosive charges up to the gunners. Rogers ordered each powder monkey to carry the charges under their jackets as a further precaution against flying sparks.

Dawn on 22 December and Rogers peered through the gloom, heartened by what he saw. During the calm night, the *Dutchess* had managed to come to within two miles of the galleon and the *Duke* three. As a morning breeze sprung up Rogers knew he was in a better position than the *Dutchess* so he ordered the sails to be raised to their maximum in order to catch the wind that was now behind them. Moving faster than the *Dutchess*, the *Duke* was bearing down on the galleon while the *Dutchess* had the wind against her. 'I ordered a large kettle of chocolate to be made for our ship's company having no spirituous liquor to give them, and then went to prayers, but before we had concluded, were disturb'd by the enemy firing at us,' Rogers wrote in his diary.

With the boom from the Spanish guns the *Duke*'s snipers ran from their kneeling positions at prayer up into their stations in the rigging while the gunners moved quickly to their gun posts waiting for their gun captains to give them the word to fire. Over and over Rogers had drilled his gun crews, in mock battles with the other ships, or just as exercises, to work as a team, efficiently and effectively. But while the *Duke* was moving in on the galleon only the enemy ship's stern guns and the *Duke*'s bow guns were firing and that was at extreme range.

Rogers planned his tactics, quickly analyzing the situation. He knew the galleon was in a difficult position because his faster frigate was overtaking her on her windward side. If the Spaniard remained on the same course as Rogers and if the wind remained in his favour, being in the faster vessel, he knew he would be able to manoeuvre the *Duke* as he liked. So he waited for the inevitable evasive action from the Spanish ship to plan his next moves.

The slightest movement of the enemy's yard-arms would tell him which way the enemy vessel was going to go; so Rogers kept his eyes fixed on them. But the Spanish ship did not try to take any evasive action, did not cut across Rogers's bow to try to pick up the wind and outrun him or turn and fight. Instead, it held to the same course, the captain probably thinking that his 500-ton galleon with over fifty guns was more than a match for the puny frigate quickly gaining on him.

Rogers's heart must have been soaring. He could hardly believe his eyes. The enemy captain was handing him a chance to win a decisive and quick battle by executing a tactic that most captains can only dream of but rarely ever get the chance to carry out. This could be the highlight of his entire seafaring career. There was no way he would let this opportunity slip by him.

From each yard-arm the Spaniards had hung barrels which Rogers assumed were full of gunpowder designed to stop them from boarding her. 'The enemy firing her stern chase several times, we returned it with our forchase.' As they drew closer to the ship the gunners fired the forward guns of the *Duke*'s broadside battery. Gun crews worked feverishly, loading their cannon and ramming the shot down the barrels, pushing the cannon back into their ports as the gun captains ordered them to fire, firing one gun after the other as the *Duke* drew abreast of the galleon. Gradually, the *Duke* brought all its guns to bear on the Spanish vessel until both ships were parallel and firing broadsides at each other at point-blank range. Thickening, choking smoke from the roaring guns filled the air, shrouding both ships with a black gloom while above the whine of shot, the splintering of wood and the ripping of sails came the whip-crack sounds of small arms fire as the snipers in the rigging of both ships opened fire, trying to pick off the officers on the decks of each ship. 'They returned as thick for awhile,' Rogers continued. 'But they did not ply their guns so fast as we.'

Rogers had brought the *Duke* to point-blank range for a reason: he was risking everything in order to end the battle quickly and bring the Spanish galleon to her knees. But he had to be close to execute the manoeuvre he had in mind. He was fighting her with wind and sails as well as with guns.

Suddenly a twelve-pound shot smashed into the *Duke*'s mizzenmast and split it. Rogers stared up at it for a few minutes, holding his breath. If it came down then that was the end, not just of victory but of the whole expedition and those that survived would probably end up prisoners of the Spanish. A

The street where Rogers's house stood in Queen Square Bristol as it is today. (*Author's collection*)

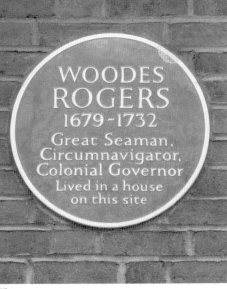

WOODES
ROGERS
1679~1732
Great Seaman,
Circumnavigator,
Colonial Governor
Lived in a house
on this site

This photograph, taken from the centre of the square, shows the building bearing a plaque that commemorates Rogers and his house which stood in this spot. (*Author's collection*)

A view of the Bristol dockyards today. Even now there are masts to be seen in a replica galleon tied up near the SS *Great Britain*. (*Author's collection*)

Another view of the docks today: Rogers's house in Queen Square was only a short walk to the docks. Though today the masts of large sailing vessels are gone we can imagine what it must have been like. (*Author's collection*)

The *Duke* sets sail: an illustration of the *Duke* leaving the docks in Bristol for the round the world voyage.

The *Duke* rounds the Horn: the *Duke* and *Dutchess* round Cape Horn in appalling weather in order to get into Pacific waters to plunder the Spanish vessels sailing from Manila to Acapulco.

Selkirk comes aboard: Lord Selkirk was found by Rogers stranded on Juan Fernández Island and his rescue and subsequent story formed the basis for the famous yarn *Robinson Crusoe* by Daniel Defoe.

Careening the *Duke*: throughout the voyage, Rogers regularly careened both the *Duke* and the *Dutchess* in order to get as much speed as possible from both the little frigates. (*Copyright by Dav* *Barlow reprinted by kind permission*)

Attacking the galleon: this illustration shows the *Duke* i action against the first Manil ship which proved to be loa with treasure.

Battle on the deck: snipers fire on a Spanish vessel as the *Duke* closes in for the capture. (*Copyright by David Barlow reprinted by kind permission*)

rs is wounded: during the action against the Manila ship Rogers was wounded, a shot hitting
n the jaw. But while lying on the deck bleeding he continued to give orders by writing them out.

ng the Manila ship: this illustration shows the unsuccessful attempt by Rogers to take the
nd, much larger Manila ship. (*Copyright by David Barlow reprinted by kind permission*)

Aerial view of Fort Charlotte: this fort overlooking Nassau was rebuilt several years after Rogers' second stint as governor of the Bahamas. (*Printed by kind permission of the Bahamas Ministry of Tourism*)

Another view of Fort Charlotte on New Providence Island near Nassau. (*Printed by kind permission of the Bahamas Ministry of Tourism*)

ther view of Fort Charlotte, showing how it must have looked when Rogers was governor.
ted by kind permission of the Bahamas Ministry of Tourism)

ernment House: Rogers had Government House built while he was governor of the Bahamas
this is how it looks today. (*Printed by kind permission of the Bahamas Ministry of Tourism*)

A computer drawing showing what is left of the ruins of the old fort at Nassau. (*Printed by kind permission of the Bahamas Ministry of Tourism*)

This hut, though built for tourists, is a good example of what the huts on the island must have looked like when Rogers first arrived at Nassau as governor. (*Printed by kind permission of the Bahamas Ministry of Tourism*)

religious man, he must have prayed for it to stay put. The mast did hold, and he turned his attention back to the enemy vessel. Still sailing faster than the galleon, his sails fully raised, he was now yard-arm to yard-arm with the galleon, his men in the rigging taking shots at the Spanish crew. He ordered the *Duke* to be moved so that it blocked the wind from the galleon, acting like a wall so that no wind could hit the Spaniard's sails. That was his plan – and it worked.

With the wind gone, the enemy's sails fell limp and she started dropping back, losing speed while the *Duke*, her sails full, kept moving ahead. Now would come the test and Rogers could taste victory.

Bullets flew thick and fast on both sides. Some whined and whizzed past Rogers's head, smashing into the deck, splintering the wood. Splinters from smashed gunwhales and wooden railings flew around the deck. Suddenly, Rogers felt a sting in his cheek, followed by a spike of agony as he spun around and fell to the deck. The ball had gone through his left cheek tearing away a large part of his upper jaw and knocking several of his teeth on to the deck. 'I was forced to write what I would say, to prevent the loss of blood and because of the pain I suffered by speaking,' he later entered into his journal.

Instead of rolling around the deck screaming, he calmly gathered his inner strength and with a shaking hand scrawled out the final orders of the battle that would seal the galleon's fate. His orders were for the crew to take the *Duke* forward until it was just barely clear of the galleon, which was now floundering without wind in its sails, then they were to come quickly about and bring the *Duke* directly across the Spaniard's bow, raking it with cannon fire then coming around down the other side continuing to plaster the enemy vessel with cannon fire.

Well trained, his crew carried out his orders. From his prostrate position on the deck he felt the ship turn. The gunners wasted no time as the *Duke* came across the galleon's bow. They were so close to the enemy ship that their cannon tore into her using her broadside to rake her from bow to stern. Below decks, sweating smoke-stained crews worked with precision. Switching to the deadly cans full of shrapnel they fired again and again. Flames shot from their guns that recoiled against restraining tackle, were quickly sponged down, reloaded and hauled back into position and fired again.

On the enemy's decks, the iron bits and rusty nails ripped into the men and rigging, mauling and shredding them as if they were paper. Men were cut down by the flying debris that was almost red-hot. They screamed as the iron scraps tore into their flesh. Rigging was ripped and torn, the limp sails shredded and the masts peppered with flying shrapnel. If they stood and fought they would be cut down since their gun crews had been blasted to silence by the combination of cannon shot and flying shrapnel and all that was left were their bow guns.

Rogers had carried out a masterful tactic, showing the Spanish that superior firepower meant nothing against superior tactics and seamanship. He pushed the galleon into a position where it lost the wind and then made his move, bringing his guns to bear where they would be the most effective. The gunners did the rest 'and ply'd them so warmly, that she soon struck her colours, two-thirds down.'

Finally, the *Dutchess* caught up and fired five volleys of small shot at the galleon; these missed, but the effort was wasted as she had already surrendered to the *Duke*. 'This galleon was called by the long name of *Nostra Signiora de la Encarnación Desengano*,' Rogers noted. 'Sir John Pitchburty, Commander, she had twenty guns with twenty patereroes and 193 men, whereof nine were killed, ten wounded and several blown up and burnt with powder.' The only other casualty onboard the *Duke* was an Irishman, who was slightly wounded.

Instead of letting the surgeons see to him, Rogers immediately scribbled an order for the *Duke*'s pinnace to bring him the commander of the galleon. Pitchburty, or Jean Presbert, was an influential Frenchman who had been allowed to command the galleon as a point of honour. He had little experience in fighting battles at sea. Once he was rowed over and presented to the wounded Rogers he was able to tell his captor news that at once sounded positive but later turned out to be a mixed blessing.

The Spanish in Manila had accurate intelligence reports, much more so than those of the Viceroy of Peru. These reports told them of two small English ships sailing in the South Seas looking to intercept the treasure ships from Manila to Acapulco. So rather than send out the customary single galleon the Spanish had sent two. The one Rogers captured, the *Encarnación*, was the smaller; the other, the *Begonia* was huge and the faster of the two. The *Encarnación* had left Manila in the company of the *Begonia* but had lost sight of her three months before and Pitchburty assumed she had reached Acapulco before they did.

As profit was their main goal on this voyage, the chance for them to capture an even bigger prize could not be missed. But first arrangements were made to have the smaller galleon secured so they could chase the bigger one. The *Encarnación*, its crew and passengers were escorted by the *Duke* and *Dutchess* into Port Seguro to the loud cheering from the crews of the *Marquis* and the

Jesus, Maria y José, where they were secured by some of the men from the *Duke*. By now the *Marquis* was fit for sailing and she, along with the *Dutchess*, headed out to sea to find the bigger galleon.

On 24 December, a few days after Rogers had received his wound, he wrote in his journal: 'In the night I felt something clog my throat, which I swallowed with much pain, and suppose it was part of my jaw bone or the shot which we can't yet give account of. But I soon recovered myself only my throat and head being greatly swelled; I have much ado to swallow all sorts of liquid for sustenance, which made me very weak and that I spoke in great pain and not loud enough to be heard at any distance.' Rogers was unable to resist the temptation to go after the bigger prize despite the protestations of the surgeons and his chief officers who wanted him to rest aboard the *Encarnación*, (which was later renamed the *Batchelor*).

A meeting was called on the morning of 24 December to decide if they should go for the *Begonia*. Rogers was expecting a negative result, but it was positive. Everyone wanted to go for the much bigger prize. Rogers felt that their only hope of taking her lay in boarding the *Begonia*, and if they concentrated their heaviest firepower he felt they could fight their way to come alongside the galleon and land boarding parties. His feeling was that the *Duke* and the *Dutchess* could do the job the best with most of the crew of the *Marquis* making up the boarding parties.

Rogers knew the *Marquis* was a clumsy vessel to handle and it could, with a skeleton crew, stay to guard the *Encarnación*; but Captain Courtney and his officers aboard the *Dutchess* along with Captain Cooke commanding the *Marquis* were having none of it. Courtney wanted to prove that the *Dutchess* was equally as good a fighting ship as the *Duke* and Cooke wanted to get in on the action now that the *Marquis* was re-rigged and ready to fight. Both men believed they could take on the large *Begonia* without any help from the *Duke*.

So Rogers's battle plan was rejected in favour of a plan that ordered the squadron's worst ship and the weakest of the two frigates out to fight an enemy vastly superior in all ways – there was nothing Rogers could do about it. The Bristol merchants who backed the expedition had demanded that majority rule must apply. 'So the officers of our consorts being agreed, and making up the majority of our council, we were obliged to stay in the harbour much against our will.'

The committee also decided to take the *Encarnación* back to England. Some of the crew were Filipinos and forty of them were hired to help man her for the voyage home. The committee also agreed that the remaining 170 Spanish prisoners were to be transferred to the *Jesus, Maria y José* to set sail for Acapulco after the plunder that vessel was carrying had been transferred to the *Duke*'s hold. The *Duke*, the committee agreed, was to remain in the harbour at Puerto Seguro guarding the treasure ship.

On Christmas Eve 1709 the *Dutchess* and the *Marquis* set sail to search for the *Begonia*. Once they had left Rogers was not content just to sit back and do nothing because he was worried his two sister ships would be pounded into oblivion. Placing two lookouts on a hill to the seaward of the harbour he instructed them to wave signal flags when they caught sight of the *Begonia*. He then took the remaining crew of the *Encarnación* and put them all onto the *Jesus, Maria y José* which he moved out and anchored in deep water, removing the rudder and sails to turn it into a prison ship. The 170 Spanish prisoners were guarded by a handful of English men while on the *Encarnación*, Rogers put twenty-two men to guard the treasure ship and ensure it was secured. Rogers was now free to wait for the signals and try to join his sister ships already at sea. He did not have long to wait.

On the afternoon of 26 December 'two sentries who had been placed upon a hill above the port signalled by three waffs that a third sail was in sight, as well as the *Dutchess* and *Marquis*.' Rogers decided to rejoin the *Duke* and left Captain Dover in charge of and keeping a watchful eye on the *Encarnación*.

By seven in the evening the *Duke* was under way as darkness closed in, and by daybreak all three ships were sighted to windward but the wind was so slight that Rogers and his crew could only just stand by while the *Marquis* and the *Dutchess*, nearly four leagues away, engaged the enemy ship. He was itching to get up and join the fight but without the wind there was little he could do. However, by midnight the *Duke* joined the other two ships and Rogers discovered that the *Marquis* had fired almost all its powder and shot, with almost no effect on the much bigger Spanish galleon. Her guns were just too small to make any difference. Peppered with shot from the galleon the *Dutchess* had to turn away, with several men wounded in the engagement, and to make repairs to her foremast as well as try to repair all the damage done, especially from receiving a shot in the powder-room.

'Curiously enough,' Rogers wrote, 'the Spaniard had been making signals to the *Duke* and edging towards her all day, mistaking her for her lost consort, until just before dusk, otherwise, having little wind and that against us, we should not have been up with her at all.'

The following day Rogers was finally in position to join in the fight, only to discover that his six-pound cannon had no effect on the *Begonia*. Rogers says in his journal that the ship was well provided for close-quarter fighting, with strong barriers of wood across the ship in certain places used as a retreat when being boarded with ports in them for small arms fire. In addition to this it had boarding-netting, strong netting extending the length of the vessel up to the height of the rigging to prevent the enemy from jumping aboard from their own rigging.

Things aboard the *Dutchess* were going badly. They now had twenty men killed or wounded while on the *Duke* a fireball landing on the quarterdeck started a fire. But before men could throw buckets of water at it an ammunition chest caught fire. Men shouted and screamed and suddenly it exploded, sending debris and fire in all directions and severely burning Mr Vanbrugh and a Dutchman.

Again, Rogers was badly wounded. 'Just before we blew up on the quarterdeck I was unfortunately wounded in the left foot by a splinter, part of my heel bone being struck out and my ankle being cut above half through which bled very much before it could be dressed, and weaken'd me so that I could not stand but had to lay on my back in great misery.'

For almost seven hours the three little ships attacked, harried and harassed the Spanish galleon, firing more than 500 shot, but the much larger ship continued onwards, pounding the British ships with its 60 twelve-pound cannon. All their firing had done was to shatter the enemy's rigging and kill two of their men in the crow's nest lookouts on the tops of their mainmasts.

'Having our rigging very much shattered,' Rogers wrote in his journal, 'we sheered off and brought to, making a signal to our consorts to consult what to do. Meanwhile, we got fishes for support to the mast and fasten'd it as well as we could. Capts. Courtney and Cooke came aboard and we considered the condition of our three ships were in, their masts and rigging being much damaged and we in a place where we could get no replacements. If we engaged the enemy again we could do no more than we had already done, and t'was evident we did her no great hurt, because we saw few of our shot enter her sides to any purpose. Also, the least jolt in the world would bring our mainmast and the *Dutchess*'s foremast down, either of which by its fall might carry away another mast. Then we should be like a target for the Spaniard, so that by his great guns he might either sink or take us and then go into the harbour and take possession of the treasure ship we had.'

It did not take long for them to make a decision, which was 'that after keeping the galleon company till night they should then lose her, and return to the harbour to look after the prize already taken.' This was not just a decision of common sense but in some ways of self-preservation. All three vessels had taken a pounding from the galleon. They had a long voyage across the Pacific and round the Cape of Good Hope ahead of them and, without the *Dutchess*'s foremast and the *Duke*'s mainmast, the voyage at best could have had a long delay and at worst could have been completely doomed.

The following morning, 28 December, the Spanish galleon had gone, sailed during the night on to Acapulco, to presumably boast about their great victory. The *Begonia* had not come away unscathed: her sails and rigging had been shattered and her mizzen-yard shot down during the fight with two of her men killed. The English themselves had nothing to be ashamed of. They had been defeated in this battle but the voyage was for profit and not for glory, and back in Seguro lay a prize worth a fortune.

As the crews repaired their ships, the officers began to study the *Encarnación*'s cargo and discovered she was carrying items such as jewelled snuff boxes, rich tapestries, pearls, priceless china made for Queen Maria Luisa of Spain, laced ivory fans, embroidered silk gowns, more than a thousand pairs of silk stockings, chests of musk for perfume, tons of rare spices, delicate Chinese silks and exotic Oriental textiles. Such silks and textiles, as we have said before, were scarce in Europe. One thing Rogers and the rest of his officers knew was that the plunder from the *Encarnación* was probably worth millions on the English market. So the defeat to the *Begonia* seemed much less painful.

Chapter 8

Bad Blood

Bad blood had been brewing for some time between Captain Dover and Rogers. Rogers never forgave him for his cautiousness at Guayaquil which, he believed, cost them a massive fortune. As they left the port of Seguro that bad blood once again started to flow.

Rogers was now prostrate and in misery from the wounds to his jaw and to his ankle. A new commander had to be appointed for the *Batchelor* (*Encarnación*) and Captain Dover was selected by the majority for this post, utterly against Rogers's wishes. As before, his selection was based on his having the largest investment in the ships and because he was President of the Council, not because he had the necessary experience. But Rogers's protests this time did not go unheeded. In his journal he wrote about 'how it was now after taking this rich prize our great misfortune to have a paper war amongst ourselves'. Rogers had a very low opinion of Dover, as he stated plainly: 'Owing to his violent temper, capable men could not well act under him, while as a Dr of physick he was incapable as a seaman himself.' Rogers should know. He was very likely the recipient of Dover's treatment, which we can only guess at.

Peace was declared between the two sides when Rogers's first lieutenant, Robert Frye, and William Stretton were appointed to take sole charge of the *Batchelor*, the new name for the recently acquired galleon which they had renamed (after one of the backers of the expedition) and refitted as best they could at Puerto Seguro. Both these men were to have sole charge of the navigation and running of the ship, while Selkirk and another man were appointed as chief mates, which left Captain Dover in charge of everything else.

Thirty good men were sent across from the *Duke*, twenty-five from the *Dutchess* with thirteen from the *Marquis* to man the *Batchelor*, along with thirty-six Manila Indians referred to by Rogers in his journal as 'Lascarrs', and some prisoners to make up the full complement of 110 men for this large ship.

It was now 1710: the fleet set sail from Cape San Lucas in California on 11 January, heading for the island of Guam. This leg of their voyage was to take them fifty-eight days at sea, a distance of roughly 6,300 miles averaging 108 miles a day at about four and a half miles an hour. Could we in our fast and disposable society spend fifty-eight days at sea going at such a slow speed when our aircraft can do it in a few hours? That is something very few of us will ever know. But they did it, and for most of that part of the voyage Rogers lay on his back, too weak to stand. Nothing of any interest was recorded in his journal on leaving Puerto Seguro at Cape San Lucas except for several deaths of wounded and sick men.

On 14 February Rogers gathered the officers together 'in commemoration of the most ancient custom of choosing valentines. . . . I drew up a list of the fair ladies in Bristol that were in any ways related to or concerned in the ships, and sent for my officers, into the cabin, where everyone drew and drank a ladies health in a cup of punch and to a happy sight of 'em all which I did to put 'em in mind of home.'

The fight off Puerto Seguro with the large Spanish galleon had damaged the *Duke* to the extent that she now leaked constantly. The pump was still going day and night with men taking hour-long shifts to keep the water level in the ship acceptable. Each man took an hour at the pump, which in the tropical heat, especially below the decks out of the wind where it must have been stifling, would have been absolute agony for them; as Rogers wrote, 'which labour together with being on short allowance makes our people look miserably.'

Finally, on 11 March they sighted Guam. The crew of the *Duke* shouted for joy as they knew they could get the ship patched up and the pump would no longer have to be manned.

As the fleet came within sight several fast small sailing vessels came out to meet them. Rogers refers to these ships as prows, which in the Merriam-Webster online dictionary is defined as 'the main upright member at the bow of a ship'. He was so taken with these boats he called flying proahs, 'which by what I saw, I believe may run twenty miles an hour, for they passed our ships like a bird flying,' that he took one onboard the *Duke* back to London, thinking it might be a good thing to set up on the canal at St James's Park as a curiosity.

To tempt some of the crew of these fast little boats to come aboard Rogers ordered that Spanish colours be raised, which the crew quickly did. 'On turning into the harbour one prow came under our stern with two Spaniards in her,' Rogers wrote in his journal. 'Being told in Spanish in answer to their questions, that they were friends from New Spain, they willingly came onboard and enquired whether we had any letters for the Governor.' Rogers did indeed have a letter for the Governor of Guam. It stated: 'We being servants of Her

Majesty of Great Britain, stopping at these islands on our way to the East Indies, will not molest the settlement provided you deal friendly with us, being willing to pay for whatever provisions you can spare. But, if after this civil request, you do not act like a man of honour and deny us our request, you may immediately expect such military treatment as we are with ease able to give you. Signed Woodes Rogers, S. Courtney and E Cooke.'

The governor could hardly not back down. A fleet of ships had arrived in his harbour of which he knew very little. What he did know was that two of those ships appeared to be Spanish galleons and they had guns, and the ships in the rest of the fleet had guns as well. By the time he was able to mount a defence it would have been too late. The guns from the *Duke*, the *Dutchess*, the *Marquis* and the *Batchelor* could have levelled his town.

The letter had the desired effect. The Governor of Guam and his officers immediately answered with, as Rogers says in his journal, 'a present of four bullocks, one for each ship, with limes, oranges and cocoanuts. And being now arrived at a place of peace and plenty, we all became indifferent, well reconciled among ourselves after the misunderstandings at California which had been so much increased of late by our shortness of water and provisions.'

Returning the governor's generosity, the privateers entertained him and four Spanish gentlemen on the *Batchelor*, 'where we all met and made 'em as welcome as time and place would afford,' wrote Rogers, 'with music and our sailors dancing, when I, not being able to move myself, was hoisted in a chair out of my ship and the boat into the *Batchelor*.'

It is difficult to believe that he was still in an enemy port, but he had managed to establish very agreeable diplomatic relations. One can only wonder if the letter warning the Spaniards at California, New Spain and Peru about an approaching English squadron had arrived at Guam. Had they heard of the sack of Guayaquil? They did not just entertain the governor and his entourage once, but the friendly relations continued with entertainment taking place onboard the *Duke*, the *Dutchess* and the *Marquis*. In turn, the governor invited Rogers and his officers ashore to be entertained with 'sixty dishes of various sorts'. Rogers reciprocated the governor's gifts with 'two negro boys dressed in liveries together with scarlet clothe serge and six pieces of cambric'.

With stocks of Indian corn, rice and coconuts they were able to purchase fourteen small lean cattle, two cows and calves, sixty hogs and a hundred fowls. The British expedition stayed a week at Guam, at the end of which, as they were preparing to sail, Rogers released one of the first prisoners he had captured with the first prize, an old Spaniard called Antonio Gomes Figuero.

His original intention was to take this old Spaniard back to England with him to act as a witness, but the man was ill and unlikely to make the journey, 'he first signing a certificate that he saw us take certain barks and prisoners subjects to Philip V King of Spain.'

Even though they had been at Guam for a week they had not been able to completely fix the leak on the *Duke*, so for safekeeping Rogers handed a chest of plate and money to Captain Courtney to be put aboard the *Dutchess*. Still prone and unable to stand, he agreed that Courtney should take the *Dutchess* ahead of the squadron at night time. 'The *Dutchess* was to keep ahead with a light, her pinnace when possible ahead of her, all signals and tacking or altering course to be given by the *Dutchess*,' Rogers wrote.

They were to be passing through the unknown straits of Molucca, full of reefs, shoals and islands on their way to Batavia. They planned to anchor at the island of Boutong to take on wood and water before arriving at Batavia. The English knew very little of this part of the world, yet Captain Dampier had sailed these waters twice and even discovered some islands in 1699 on his last voyage there. But now he seemed to be completely lost when he tried to pilot the squadron through the straits. One can understand his lack of knowledge – more than a decade had passed since he had been there. This, with the lack of charts or maps, must have been frustrating for Rogers. Still, the squadron managed to get through after bribing the Malay skipper of a small native bark to act as their pilot between Boutong and Batavia.

The weather after leaving Guam was terrible. For several days it was dark as storms raged around them. Thunder cracked overhead and lightning flashed. The rain hammered the decks while the wind whipped up the rough seas. On 15 April they ran into three tropical showers, like giant waterspouts that smashed across the *Dutchess* first.

However, by 29 May the squadron of four ships had arrived at Boutong, where they took on water, wood and a fresh supply of fruit and vegetables. Rogers wrote an entry in his journal about the king of the island whom he described as being 'dilatory and designing in his dealings with us but we made him a present of a Bishop's cap, a thing of little use to us, but which he highly esteem'd and gratefully accepted of.'

A few days later the four ships set sail again, and on 17 June 1710 they were sailing off the north coast of Java when the *Duke* and the *Dutchess* met a Dutch ship heading east from Europe, the first such ship they had seen heading that way since the start of their expedition. The ship was a large one of 600 tons and fifty guns and it was from her officers that Rogers and his company learned that Prince George of Denmark, Queen Anne's Consort, was dead 'and that the wars continued in Europe where we had good success in Flanders, but little elsewhere.'

The cacophony of the pump being worked day and night rang in Rogers's ears as the men fought to keep the water out of the *Duke* while she still leaked. In addition to the anxiety of difficult navigation through treacherous shoals and reefs he also had to contend with a mutinous officer on the *Duke* and 'with other officers onboard the *Dutchess* which knot was only broken by putting the leaders in irons.'

On 20 June they dropped anchor in Batavia harbour. Most of the troubles he had experienced only a few days before had been smoothed over or forgotten as Rogers recorded in his journal: 'Till now I find that I was a stranger to the humours of our ship's company some of whom are hugging each other, while others bless themselves that they were come to such a glorious place for punch, where arack is eightpence per gallon, and sugar one penny a pound, whereas a few weeks past a bowl of punch to them was worth half the voyage.'

On a personal note, Rogers recorded feeling better first 'on the discovery of a large musket shot, which the doctor now cut out of my mouth, it having been there for six months, so that the upper and lower jaw being broken and almost closed, he had much ado to come at it, and that several pieces of my foot and heel bone having been removed, I believe myself, thank God, in a fair way to have the use of my foot and recover my health.'

It is hard to imagine how painful these two operations must have been. There was nothing to dull the pain at sea and, considering they were in a tropical climate with all its inherent diseases, as well as the sickness that must have been rife onboard the ships at that time, it is a wonder he survived. But that he did so is a testament to his physical, mental and emotional strength – he simply looked upon these operations as trifling discomforts.

In the harbour at Batavia they found more than forty different ships large and small and 'as customary lost almost a day in running so far west around the Globe, we here altered our account of time.' Here they began a complete overhaul of the ships and the plunder. For example, bale goods were completely rewrapped in waxcloth and tarpaulins. As they checked over each ship they found the *Marquis* to be riddled with woodworm. It was declared as unfit for the voyage home around the Cape of Good Hope and all her cargo was distributed among the other three ships. They were then able to sell the hull of the *Marquis*, which Rogers described as 'very leaky' for 575 Dutch dollars to a 'Captain John Opie of the frigate *Oley* lately arrived from London.'

Even though the Dutch were their allies they were not happy about the English ships being in their main harbour at Batavia. In contrast to Guam and other places they had visited, Rogers was not in a position to threaten the General of Batavia with his six-pounder cannon. Instead, he had to negotiate. By 8 July 'after a long correspondence and many dilatory answers,' Rogers was given permission to clean his ships at Horn Island, some three miles north of their current anchorage. The general had expressly forbidden him to clean his ships at Umrest because this was where all the Dutch ships were cleaned.

They did the best they could to keep their powder dry, as shown in an entry in the *Duke*'s log where 'in rummaging one day in the powder room we found a leak three or four feet under water which we did our best to stop.' For four months they stayed at Batavia, readying their little squadron for the journey round the Cape. In his journal Rogers describe his impressions of the island:

> *It would be too tedious to describe all the remarkable things I saw in Batavia; for I was perfectly surprised when I came hither to see such a noble city, and Europeans so well settled in the Indies; having all necessaries for building and careening ships as well as in Europe, and officers as regular as in Her Majesty's Yards; whereas we have nothing like it in India. They keep their natives under much awe but are favourable to the Chinese, who pay great rents for their shops, being about 8,000 of them who pay the Dutch a dollar a head a month for the liberty to wear their hair, which they are not allowed at home since they were conquered by the Tartars.*

However, during this time at Batavia all was not well. Rogers lost several men from fever, who had drunk foul water while careening at Horn Island. Several men at this late stage of the voyage deserted the *Duke* and the *Dutchess*, tempted by the abundance and low prices of liquor at Batavia. Having to find replacements, Rogers turned to his allies and managed to hire thirty-four Dutch sailors. In his journal he expresses great surprise at the men deserting and leaving their share of the plunder behind. Perhaps it was the prospect of continually working the pump onboard the *Duke* that was the incentive.

The little squadron did not leave Java Head until 4 October but by 27 December they were abreast of the Cape of Good Hope. During this part of the voyage nothing very remarkable took place except on 31 October when the *Duke*, 'having three feet of water in her, and her pumps choaked, we fire'd guns for our concorts to come to our relief but had just sucked her dry when the *Dutchess* came up.'

Rogers was still very thin and weak, and the day after they anchored in Table Bay at Cape Town, now in the Republic of South Africa, they buried the chief surgeon, Mr Ware, 'with naval honours as usual; being a very honest useful man, and good surgeon, bred up at Leyden in the study of phisick as well as surgery.' Mr Vanbrugh, who had caused Rogers so much trouble during the earlier part of the voyage, also died while they remained at Cape Town. During their stay in the town, the officers on the three ships spent much of their time selling their plunder and prize goods to the Dutch settlers and in one instance sold twelve black men as slaves to the Dutch.

By early April a fleet of twenty-five ships was ready to sail for Holland and it included the three English vessels. This fleet, which included sixteen Dutch East Indiamen and six English ships, was under the command of a vice and rear admiral and the commander of these merchantmen, some so large they were a thousand tons, were all officers in the Dutch navy.

Rogers was again for pushing forward rather than waiting for the convoy: 'Thinking we should lose too much time by staying for them, and the benefit of their convoy to Holland; which would not only be out of the way, but very tedious and chargeable, while having large quantities of decaying goods onboard, the time lost in waiting for the Dutch at the Cape might be better spent in Brazil, where we could lie in little danger from an enemy and vend our goods at great rates.' He goes on to say they could then sail to Bristol through the north channel during the summer 'keeping in the latitude of 55 or 56 degrees for two or three hundred leagues before getting the length or longtitude of the north of Ireland and by that means avoiding the track of an enemy.' But Rogers was again outnumbered. The majority wished to stay with the Dutch convoy rather than run any risks of losing what they had gained.

On the morning of 5 April 1711 in the picturesque harbour of Cape Town the Admiral's flagship raised a blue ensign and fired a signal for the rest of the ships to raise their anchors. However, onboard the *Duke* they raised their anchor and 'our cable rubb'd against the oakum,which for a time had partially stopped the leak, and occasioned his ship to be as leaky as ever, after having been indifferent tight for some time.' Rogers must have been furious but he had little time to think about it as the English captains were signalled to go onboard the Dutch flagship to receive their orders of sailing, which 'were very particularly and obligatory to be punctually observ'd'.

The voyage from Cape Town to Texel in Holland was in those days a long one even if the direct route was taken up the English Channel; but for a force of this size steering away across the Atlantic and not touching land with more than 5,000 men to feed, it was monotonous. Their heading westward of the Azores then north-eastward as far as the Shetlands doubled the length of the voyage.

On 14 May they crossed the equator again, which Rogers wrote in his journal was the eighth time they had done so. Travelling at around three miles an hour it took them thirty-eight days. Interestingly, the *Batchelor*, the Spanish prize, was probably the slowest ship of the fleet and Rogers had several occasions when the *Duke* had to tow her. He speaks of the Dutch admiral's civility in 'allowing her to keep ahead of the fleet at night, which he would not permit any other ship to do.' Fortunately, no disasters befell the fleet as they sailed home. The monotony of the journey was relieved for a day on 15 June 1711 when the Dutch admiral entertained the English captains and some of his Dutch officers onboard his flagship. 'The good humour of the Admiral soon made all the company understand each other without a linguist,' Rogers wrote.

As they drew further north they ran into very foggy weather, 'during which the flagship fired two guns every half hour, each ship answering with one, which consum'd a great deal of powder,' Rogers recorded in his journal. 'By the noise of the guns it was easy to keep company, though often so thick that we could not see three ships' lengths.'

On 23 July the whole squadron anchored at Texel in Holland, where he and his men were met by some of the owners who had come from England to greet him. But several delays prevented their setting sail again for the very last leg of the journey. In the company of four men of war, the *Essex*, the *Canterbury*, the *Meday* and the *Dunwich*, Rogers finally set sail for England on 14 October. He noted that 'this day, at 11 of the clock, we and our Consorts and prize got up to Eriff, where we came to an anchor, which ends our long and fatiguing voyage.'

Chapter 9

From Poverty to Governor

When the three ships, *Duke*, *Dutchess* and *Batchelor* returned from the cruising voyage round the world Rogers faced challenges in the bitter long-drawn-out disputes with the crew as well as the claims of the East India Company.

In the Pacific, as the prizes were mounting up some were suspected of privately hiding away plunder which should have gone into the common stock for even distribution to all. As we have seen, in order to restore some semblance of peace, nearly half of those on the *Duke* signed a joint agreement that, together with the threats of mutiny should they not be immediately given larger shares in the plunder, managed to keep things on an even keel. The agreed shares for the agents and the interpreter were cut and substantial amounts of what was due to Rogers and Captain Courtney had also to be given away in order for this peace to hold.

Three months later the trouble exploded again as suspicions remained amongst the crew despite the hard and fast agreements made earlier. After the taking of the *Encarnación* the crew believed her cargo to be worth far more than it was. Agitators among the crew kept them at a fever pitch, winding them up to believe that the cargo of silks onboard this Spanish ship was worth far more than its actual market value. Indeed, the sailors aboard the *Duke* and the *Dutchess* believed the total value of the proceeds of the voyage amounted to some three million pounds, and this, they believed included the amount embezzled or hidden away by the officers. Even the officers had disputes between them as the ships sailed back home for England.

But events took a turn for the worse when an individual named Creagh named himself as an agent for the men. With 5 per cent as his fee, more than 200 of the men voted for him. Once they were in London Creagh mounted several legal delays and managed to stop the ships being cleared of their cargoes. The case escalated and was eventually heard in Chancery; and once the cargo had been sold the still unpaid sailors twice petitioned the House of Lords, accusing the officers of embezzlement. The wrangling went on for five years and the expenses piled up until at last the officers and the men got their share of the £50,000 that was left.

Rogers himself received such a poor reward for the leadership and skill he had shown during the voyage that his total takings did not amount to more than £1,600[26] total and in the three years he had been away he had become bankrupt, probably because of the debts his wife had incurred while she remained in Bristol. He was tired and disillusioned.[27]

By the time Rogers returned Admiral Whetstone had passed away and his wife remained living in her house at St Michael's Hill, with her step-daughter to keep her company. The two houses in Queen Square were not used by either the Whetstones or the Rogerses and, after the death of Lady Whetstone, passed to Admiral Whetstone's son-in-law, the Bristol merchant David Goizin.

Rogers remained in Bristol for some little while: we know this because there the birth of his fourth son was recorded, the son to carry the family name of Woodes, in August 1712; but less than a year later the child was buried in the churchyard of St Michael, having passed away in April of 1713.

Rogers knew that he had to restore his fortunes and had his eye on a voyage to the pirate-ridden island of Madagascar. The Rogers family may have had some knowledge of Madagascar: as we already know, they knew William Dampier, whose book of 1699 contains passages describing the tides, geography, people of the place, and Dampier writes that the geographical information was given to him by his friend Captain Rogers, whom he describes as being a very ingenious person and well experienced on that coast. Dampier includes descriptions of Natal, of the bushmen and Zulus as told to him by this Captain Rogers.

Though Rogers was a common surname, it is possible that he may have been Woodes Rogers's father. Both Dampier, the famous navigator, and Rogers the seaman of Poole could have met because of their common associations with life in Dorset. Between his voyages Dampier spent his time ashore on his brother's farm in North Porton near Bridport and used to take long breaks along the Dorset coast. It is highly likely that he made friends all along the county's coast, and this could explain why the famous Dampier could so readily serve under the Poole captain's son, our hero Woodes Rogers.

Pirates were the main problem with his new venture of settling the southern part of Madagascar in an orderly way. This region was wild, untouched, a no man's land filled with pirates living in an anarchistic commonwealth. Ships from India, the Far East and Mocha filled with coffee beans for the London coffee-houses were ripe targets for these outlaws. English, Dutch, Portuguese or Arab, they were all targets to the pirates.

To finance the voyage to Madagascar Rogers returned to his backers in the

East India Company. He had chosen a merchantman of some 460 tons named *Delicia*. The necessary capital and permissions were obtained by Rogers for the voyage and he made an affidavit saying that the voyage was for the purpose of buying slaves for the East Indies. The owners and backers of the expedition picked the crew, making sure that none were of weak temperament who might turn to the pirates rather than stay with their ship and captain. So in late 1713 the *Delicia* set sail from London and early the following year landed at Cape Town before moving on to Madagascar. Here Rogers spent two months, and by May 1714 had returned to the Cape.

It was here that he heard that a Dutch ship had been taken in 1712 by the French and that more than eighty of her crew were stranded on the Africa-facing side of Madagascar. Many had died but the remaining fifty were said to be building a sloop to turn pirate and join the ranks of the outlaws hiding and using the coastal parts of the island, ready to pounce on the East India ships plying those waters.

Rogers did not just want to stop the reinforcement of the pirates, he wanted to eliminate them altogether. The poor natives they had settled amongst hated them and their half-caste children. For years they did not even have a ship to carry out robbery at sea. Instead of going after them, Rogers contacted the pirates to give hope to those who were English by telling them to repent their evil ways and take advantage of the pardon offered by the crown so that they could go into respectable seafaring trades. Persuading them to draw up a petition to the queen for clemency, he told them to assure their sovereign that they were longing to come home.

By the time he returned to England in 1715 Rogers had begun planning a well-ordered pirate-free and peaceful Madagascar settlement. He believed that such a colony would be as good for the English as the provisioning station at the Cape had been for the Dutch. Lucrative, profitable and above all influential, the station would add another feather in the English cap, ensure more secure trade routes and especially add a thorn in the side of the French and the Spanish.

But to set up any kind of peaceful settlement there the pirates had to go. Extermination or conversion were two possible solutions. Conversion seemed to be uppermost in his mind. We know this because he wrote twice to the Society for Promoting Christian Knowledge asking for a consignment of books for what he called the English inhabitants of Madagascar – that is, the pirates.[28] The books duly arrived and he was ready to mount his attempt to return to Madagascar to convert the pirates. However, nothing came of his idea to settle

Madagascar, and he never went back there.

Without Madagascar, Rogers turned his attention to another place that was filled with pirates – the Bahamas. Again, placing an English settlement on these islands that would be secure, safe and thriving with trade would bring more cash into English merchants as well as the government and provide another chance to get at the Crown's enemies.

This far-flung group of low-lying islands in the West Indies was a vital link for maintaining communications by sea from the British plantations to the Spanish Main. The islands were on the route that ships sailed on their way home to Europe or on their way down from New England, Virginia and New York. There are dozens of islands that make up the Bahamas, and in the centre was one that had an anchorage that the rest of them lacked. This was the island of Providence. Nearby Cuba and Florida were Spanish colonies. The Spanish also laid claim to the Bahamas, but for decades had not been able to enforce their claims, so the islands were under the nominal rule of the British, who claimed possession.

King Charles II had made six Lord Proprietors rulers of the American and West Indian colonies in his stead rather than directly appoint governors. Three of those Lords included the Earl of Craven, Lord Berkeley and the Duke of Albemarle, and it was their duty to appoint governors to their islands. However, there was very little real rule there and the peace of the place depended on the governors themselves. The governor in 1689 was a strict and sober man, Thomas Bridges, who preached a sermon every Sunday and fired a gun from the little fort overlooking the harbour known as Nassau.

The Spanish from Cuba mounted several attacks, and early in the War of Succession the settlement was destroyed by the Spanish and the French and left to the pirates, who had their own rule of conduct and created their own bloody, unlawful and violent society using the ruins of the settlement as their base to attack the shipping plying the waters around the islands. From the ashes of the old Providence a ramshackle, shambles of a settlement was built by the pirates. This became a thorn in the side of the British as the pirates began to spread their wings, becoming a real danger to South Carolina, which was much more important to the Lord Proprietors.

New Providence, as it was then called, was the scene of debauchery and drunken lewd society. Indeed, the vacuum created by the inability of the British to assert their sovereignty over the islands meant that others such as the Spanish and the French were ready enough to take on the challenge.

In 1717 the Ostend East India Company was opened as the way into the Far

Eastern trade routes by the Austrian Netherlands (now Belgium), another problem for England. One of its promoters, a Scotsman named John Ker of Kersland, was an adventurer and had ideas of his own. In his memoirs he wrote that his plan for the Bahamas was to create a West Indian emporium under the colours of imperial Austria which would threaten everyone else already involved in American trade. The idea was for the Austrian emperor to declare New Providence a free port for all nations, which would bring in all types of settlers and religions. But he never got a chance to realize his plans as the Ostend Company fell victim to arguments, politics and rivalries.

Whether these influences or others had an effect on the government of George I is difficult to say with real certainty, for while these events were going on, Woodes Rogers and his influential friends were busy trying to influence the government to act by setting up a peaceful settlement and ridding the place of pirates. Rogers spent most of his time in London with his friends, one of the most influential of whom was Joseph Addison, Secretary of State for the Southern Department and the man who would be able to handle the papers needed to make improvements on the island of New Providence.

In 1714 the Governor of Bermuda complained to the Crown that the Bahamas were completely lawless and that no settlers would go there unless there was a safe, decent and lawful settlement. In the Calendar of State Papers (Colonial) America and West Indies series there is an entry concerning John Graves, the unpaid Bahaman collector of customs, who put in a plea for a garrison and settlement with himself as the governor to take direct control of the little colony away from the absent Lord Proprietors. However, the lords decided to nominate one Roger Mostyn as the governor, but at the end of 1715 the council of Trade and Plantations wrote to the king indicating their displeasure and surprise that the Lord Proprietors, so long absent from the scene, should decide to nominate a governor now. They felt, according to the Calendar of State Papers, that the English government should take back control of the Bahamas and directly appoint the governor. Mostyn was appointed by the king but no records show he ever ventured near the place. In 1717 the council of Trade and Plantations began discussions with the leading merchants in the American and Plantation trades. The discussions centred around the fact that the pirates now infested the waters around the West Indies and North America, threatening the vital trade routes. It was recommended that protection be sent at once. It was suggested by the traders that the pirates should be given pardons; Joseph Addison began drafting conditions to tempt the pirates to accept the pardons and work for the Crown.

Rogers and his friends had been at work for several months on the plan to set up a settlement with a garrison in the Bahamas. Colonial Office papers corroborate this and include the basis on which Rogers built his case. Economic resources such as brazilletto wood, tortoiseshells, whale oil and any treasure taken from Spanish ships was included in the proposal by Rogers and his backers and friends. To give weight to the proposal, Rogers enclosed letters signed by influential people and by the traders who were losing their profits to the marauding pirates. One of the letters had fifty-seven signatures including Micajah Perry, an influential City merchant who eventually became an MP. Other signatures included William Fauquier, whose son became the Lieutenant Governor of Virginia. Another letter bore thirty-four signatures describing Rogers as having created very advantageous proposals and being a person of integrity and very loyal to the king's government. Another letter had seventy-nine signatures from leading Bristol merchants, a cross-section of the commercial elite of the time from that port city.

The main body of the petition stated that the Bahamas had been suspended for a long time between the Lord Proprietors and His Majesty's government. Citing his experience in 'remote undertakings' to add more weight to his argument, Rogers asked to be commissioned by the king as governor and hoped for 'success in this task of sound colonisation'.

The proposal was steered through official channels by Rogers's friend Joseph Addison and after some time the king granted Rogers his commission as governor and commander of the military garrison but did not grant him a salary. Once there he was forced to use his own money, which led to his ruin.

The Lord Proprietors were relieved of their civil and military rule over the Bahamas and, according to Colonial Office papers, agreed readily to this because they realized that having the area cleaned up and free of pirates would benefit their much larger and more lucrative holdings in South Carolina.

Rogers was left to bankroll most of the expedition himself. He put some £3,000 of his own money into it while six other backers spent about £11,000 equipping the expedition, which was to set sail in the spring of 1718. Also, they set up an independent company of infantrymen mostly taken from the ranks of the outpatients of Chelsea Hospital as well as from regiments on guard duty in England and Ireland. Rogers offered to feed and equip these soldiers from his own pocket in order to reduce the strain on state funds.

Colonial and State Office papers also indicate that provisions were made for the civilian settlers who would be needed to counter the pirates not by violence but by setting up a steady, sober and peaceful settlement where there was no place for the pirates and their debauchery. Some 500 refugees, known as Palatines, persecuted German Protestants from the Palatinate, were lined up for the journey though many went to mainland America instead. According to the Colonial Office papers, assumptions were made that salaries would be found for teachers and pastors while £2,500 was set aside for corn, cattle, seeds and implements. To transport all this, the ship was one Rogers already knew – the *Delicia*.

So in mid–April 1718 the *Delicia* weighed anchor and joined up with Captain Chamberlain commanding the thirty-two gun *Milford*, the commodore's ship of the little squadron detailed to escort Rogers and his settlers to the Bahamas.

Picking up the wind and setting course, Rogers must have felt pride as he paced the quarterdeck of the *Delicia*, looking out at the squadron escorting him on the epic journey that would change his career forever.

Chapter 10

The New Governor

Nassau, today's capital of the Bahamas, is located on the island of New Providence, a regularly shaped island approximately fifteen by six miles. The highest ground is formed by the low ridges that run along its length and never reach more than 100 feet. The capital is on the northern side of the island, whose lovely natural harbour is shielded by the long, low Harbour Island. The islets, Silver Cay and Long Cay, continue after Harbour Island in a rough line towards the west. Between Harbour Island, Silver Cay and Long Cay and the main island is a channel that in Rogers's day was deep enough for large sailing men-of-war to enter the main anchorage opposite the town and anchor there. In the east there was another way in or out which for the pirates was called the East Passage and was an excellent way of escaping if necessary. It is at the narrowest point between the main island and Harbour Island, near Potters Cay, where a skilful navigator could guide a ship through the narrow passage. At the time of Rogers's arrival at his new posting only the islands of Abaco, Eleuthera and Harbour Island were inhabited.

His voyage took three months, and he was in the company of the *Milford* and two naval sloops, the *Rose* and the *Shark*, which provided security against pirates whom it would be too hard for the *Delicia* to fight off on her own. The *Rose* was sent ahead to provide intelligence of the pirates and find pilots who could navigate the waters between the many shoals and cays for the larger ships of the small expedition.

After stopping in St Kitts and Anguilla, Rogers and the rest of the ships except the *Rose* dropped anchor on 24 July 1718 just outside Nassau, the pirates' harbour. We know from Colonial Office papers held in the National Archives and also from the captain's log of the *Milford* that the *Delicia* and the warships paused just outside the entrance of the harbour. The place was bleak. The town was simply a mixture of ramshackle huts, shacks and tents. There was no wharf and the harbourside fort was a crumbling and dilapidated structure so badly built that when a bastion collapsed some time after Rogers's arrival it was discovered that the building had rotted to its foundation. The taverns and shore buildings of the pirates were the most prominent structures.

The pirates had scattered their rubbish all over the beach and the waterfront and the place stank from rotting hides, according to the captain's log of the *Milford*.

The people themselves were largely pirates, a disorderly, unwashed bunch of cutthroats. Thomas Walker, the governor nominated by the Lord Proprietors years before, had originally fled the islands for fear of his life and his family's, and because of his ill-treatment by the pirates he now returned with Rogers. The only official on the island was the cantankerous, bedridden old man, John Graves, who lived in utter squalor in the only building that even remotely resembled a house and had an annual salary of £70 for collecting non-existent customs revenues from the pirates who paid no revenue whatsoever. As far as inhabitants were concerned, there were only a few hundred legitimate settlers and the rest were pirates.

The majority of these outlaws were ordinary seamen who had a great distaste for ordered life and especially for the life of a settler, tilling the land. In times of war it is likely that most of these ordinary seamen would have been aboard a naval ship fighting the Spanish or French.

As darkness fell and the little fleet waited just outside the harbour some local men from Harbour Island came aboard the *Delicia* bringing news that there were more than a thousand pirates on the shore waiting for them. The leaders of the pirates were Henry Jennings, Benjamin Hornigold, Thomas Burgess and Charles Vane. Before Rogers's arrival the most notorious pirate of all, Blackbeard Edward Teach, had shipped out, leaving the rest to face Rogers. They would cause problems that would almost overwhelm him.

These leaders waited in or around the town of Nassau, the men from Harbour Island advised Rogers. They also told him the fort was in such a bad state of repair that it only had one gun mounted, a nine-pounder. There was no accommodation for the men except for the only official house, which was already inhabited by John Graves. The rest of the huts and tents were for the pirates.[29]

Captain Thomas Whitney of the *Rose* decided to brave the pirates and headed into the harbour. The *Rose*, accompanied by the *Shark*, both with pilots who knew the waters, sailed into Nassau. Most of the pirates remained quiet, except Charles Vane, who, refusing to be cowed by the show of strength swore death and perdition to the arrival of these reforming forces to tame the wild settlement. Having recently brought in a captured French ship full of loot Vane set fire to it that very night and cut the ropes tethering it, after transferring the loot to his own ship. All the guns in the ship exploded as the fire ripped through it. Whitney, believing that he was being fired at immediately lowered his pinnace and sent it ashore under the command of his lieutenant.

According to Daniel Defoe's account in *The Pyrates*, Vane captured the boat and brought the crew onboard, taking all the stores they had on the pinnace. He kept them captive until daybreak when there was enough light for him to navigate his way out of the harbour through the East Passage. Once through he hoisted his black flag and let the lieutenant, his crew and his boat go. They sailed back to the *Rose* while Vane headed for the open sea, and for the next three years he continued in his pirate ways until his death.

Finally, on 27 July 1718, after this incident had taken place, Rogers and the rest of the ships, in company with the *Milford*, entered the harbour accompanied by an eleven-gun salute from the *Rose*. The lieutenant arrived onboard, according to Defoe, and related his story to Captain Whitney, who immediately dispatched the *Buck*, an armed sloop, to chase Vane; but the pirate was long gone and the sloop returned empty-handed.

Throughout the day, the men onboard the ships stowed their sails, secured the ships and made sure each vessel was properly moored. In the morning Rogers went ashore and met the leading people of the town, including the pirate captains Hornigold, Davis, Carter, Burgess, Courant and Clark, men who, on hearing of the royal pardon decided to turn away from piracy and become respectable citizens. As Rogers landed and began to live amongst the people he came to know the different wills and personalities amongst the white settlers and the people he brought with him, a difference that he would have to face throughout his term as governor.

Upon landing, Rogers and his officers and soldiers marched straight to the broken-down fort and read out the proclamation granting Rogers rule over the settlement. After his commission the king's pardon for pirates to give up their piratical ways was also read out.

Almost immediately Rogers set about organizing the local government. Over the three-month voyage he had come to respect and trust only a few of the men on the voyage with him, and now he decided they must be in positions of authority in the new settlement. Robert Beauchamp, 2nd Lieutenant of his Company of Foot, became Secretary General. Christopher Gale became Chief Justice. William Fairfax was given the position of deputy to John Graves, the Collector of Customs, and Fairfax was content to stay as deputy with no salary and no fees until the ill-tempered, old Graves passed away.

For the rest of the posts Rogers had to turn to the inhabitants of the island, choosing the best of a bad bunch. Among the men who were living from the proceeds of the pirates, shifty, immoral men, he had to chose those with the best morals who had the least experience of or had ever had dealings with the people like Vane or Blackbeard.

Colonial Office papers, logbooks from the *Milford* and the *Rose* and committee meeting notes point to the difficulty of Rogers's task and the way in which his firmness, resolution and determination won the day. It is hard to imagine the 1,200 men and women, mostly pirates, facing down one warship, two naval sloops and an independent company of infantry. Under the steaming heat of the summer they were seeing the end of their way of life. The pirates, as we have already mentioned, were largely seamen very much like the seamen Rogers had held together during his long Pacific voyage. Looking at the *Milford*, a warship bristling with guns, small arms and full of soldiers, the pirates shifted from foot to foot knowing they had no real choice other than to accept the pardon, while others, the harder ones, fled to swell the ranks of the pirates in pirate havens such as Madagascar.

Rogers's concern was less with the hard core who had fled but the pirate seamen who had taken the pardon to remain loyal; he needed them to remain with him and not go back to their pirate ways. So the next weeks would be the most nerve-wracking time. Literature from the Society for the Promotion of Christian Knowledge was given out as a counter to the force Rogers had at his disposal. Could this be an early example of walk softly but carry a big stick?

Rogers had to do more than just threaten. His three main tasks were fortification, decent housing and cultivation. He immediately set to work on all three, even in the subtropical summer heat. The rotting hides lying neglected along the beach and waterfront gave off such a foul odour that it proved to be fatal for some of the weaker immigrants who had travelled with Rogers. He ordered the hides to be removed as soon as possible.

Sickness was rife and before houses could be constructed Rogers and his officers remained on their ships. At one time, more than a hundred men and women were ill and by November eighty had died. Many of those were the settlers who had come to dig plantations and help the Bahamas become self-sufficient agriculturally. The pirates, though reformed, were so lazy that they appeared to want to starve rather than dig to plant crops. However, Rogers did manage to get some digging started. As far as houses were concerned, Rogers ordered that sails be taken from some of the ships in the harbour and used as tents. Like Little Bristol many years before on the island of Gorgona, a tent town sprung up at Nassau to house the new arrivals. In the meantime, work was immediately begun on building proper houses. Charles Johnson, author of the

History of the Pirates, stated that settlers and pirates who had given up their illegal ways were given plots of 120 feet square and thatched cottages replaced the tents and shacks. At the same time overgrown tracks were cleared so they could become the tracks for plantations.

The fort at Nassau was something else again. Rogers's attempts to rebuild it floundered because most of the carpenters and bricklayers had died of disease and the reformed pirates were lazy and indolent. Nassau had good lime, timber and stone, but there was little chance of actually using it. Building work on the fort thus remained at a standstill. In one of his many letters to his backers in England Rogers wrote about the rebuilding of the fort and how difficult it was proving to be. A small redoubt, however, was built to guard the Eastern Passage that Vane had escaped through, and its eight guns pointed out towards the narrow dangerous waters.

Just over the horizon was Spanish Cuba. Rogers's two biggest worries were an attack from the Spanish and the pirates renouncing their pardon and renewing their old ways – since most of the worst pirates had simply slipped away. They could attack at any time. So, as Rogers wandered about the tiny settlement, personally supervising the rebuilding of the fortifications, he wondered when the pirates would come again.

One would expect the Royal Navy to have provided help to a Royal Governor; but no help came. 'There are three more of His Majesty's ships at New York that have lain there some time whilst the pirates have been very troublesome to the Carolinas and almost everywhere in the West Indies,' Rogers wrote. 'I beg if any of His Majesty's ships are ordered this way for the future, that they may be under the Direction of the Governor and council, especially whilst they are here and we may be capable to join them in serving the public.'

At this time the navy was not what it is today. Discipline was unreliable and officers often pleased themselves as to which orders they would take from their superiors. During times of peace warship commanders would often be looking out for commercial enterprise rather than strictly naval duties. Often they would carry merchandise and take high fees from merchants for doing so, using the pretence of the threat of pirates stealing the goods if they were not taken on the warship. They would arrive at their destination for a lucrative fee, so it paid the naval commanders to have pirates on the high seas during times of peace so that they could play on the fears of merchants and traders.

Governors of the American colonies were always asking the Admiralty to be stricter with their commanders, but these requests fell on deaf ears and the governors were left hoping that each commander would have the moral fibre to resist the temptations of commerce and do his duty. This met with mixed success: some commanders looked upon having their vessels as guardships, hunting pirates or just lying in anchor as impeding their commercial activities.

Every day, as worry mounted, Rogers wondered when the pirate Charles Vane would return to take the island, especially when the *Milford* and the *Rose* finally left to return to the profitable convoy runs. Commodore Chamberlain left Nassau on 16 August in the *Shark*. Many of his men had died and several others were ill, close to death. Other duties called him away. Rogers pleaded with him to allow Captain Whitney to stay on for another three weeks, and in fact he stayed for four. But bad blood between Whitney and Rogers flared up so much that by the time the *Rose* sailed out of the harbour Rogers had written many reports back to England about the behaviour of Captain Whitney, for example in his letter of early December 1718. 'It's near three months and a half since Captain Whitney Commander of His Majesty's Ship the *Rose* left me in great extremity, to go to the Havana carrying a letter from Me and some Spaniards that was left here with him and promised to return in three weeks at most, but now I hear he's got at New York and writes hither that the Spaniards design to begin with us first. The governor of the Havana takes no notice of my passes (papers) but keeps the men of this government that falls into their islands in custody. This Captain Whitney pretends he drove from the Havana to New York by stress of weather. I very much worried how it was possible he could stear clear of Providence that lies so directly in his way.' The only heavily armed vessel remaining was the *Delicia*, the ship Rogers had arrived on. Its stay was a long one, remaining to guard the harbour against pirates and sometimes acting as a prison; but it was a stay that was draining Rogers's own meagre resources and his commercial partners back in London.

Chapter 11

Rogers and the Pirates

Throughout all this time, from all the letters and reports he had written to England he heard nothing back. Not a letter, not a single word. Nothing. Feeling alone and abandoned he turned his attention to fighting the pirates before they struck again.

Many of the hard-core pirates who had taken the pardon and gone to Cuba to trade in fact had gone there to seize their vessels and begin attacking Spanish and English ships alike.

A fishing vessel out of New Providence called the *Neptune* was intercepted by Vane, who had taken it and its crew to one of the more desolate islands of the Bahamas, Green Turtle Bay, where they plundered most of its cargo of stores, partially cut the mast in half and fired a gun down its hold to try to sink her. The ball failed to go through the hull but stuck in the bilge, because the charge on the gun was insufficiently powerful. Vane gave the crew a canoe so they could get back to Nassau, and they rowed from little island to little island until another fishing boat picked them up. The crew of the *Neptune* believed Vane was still cruising in those waters. So Rogers fitted out a ship with a crew of fifty, well-armed, and sent it after Vane; but they had no luck. Instead, they did find the *Neptune* which they brought back to Nassau.

Among Charles Vane's crew was another notorious pirate, Jack Rackham, whom Vane made captain of one of his captured ships. Despite having been friends for years, the pair fell out over a quantity of liquor. Vane, discovering that his own supply was gone asked Rackham for some. Rackham gave Vane what he could spare and Vane thought it was not enough. The two men threatened each other and finally parted ways, both ready to fight. Carrying a large amount of booty, stolen from the several prizes he and Vane had taken and split between them, Rackham and several of his men decided they wanted to take the king's pardon. Using an intermediary whom they had captured, they sent to the governor of Jamaica to let them know that Rackham wanted the pardon. Unfortunately for Rackham, news of his and Vane's latest actions had reached the governor first; Rackham discovered that two well-armed sloops were out hunting for him. Instead, he made his way to New Providence and there begged Rogers to give him the royal pardon. This Rogers did. Rackham and his crew sold their goods to the local merchants and began to live the high life.

It is at this point that Rogers, albeit briefly, comes into some of the stories, legends and myths of the pirates of the Caribbean. As we have seen, England was at war with Spain and Rogers was interested in harassing Spain wherever he could. So he made the pardoned pirates privateers to go out and plunder Spanish ships and bring the booty back to Nassau, as well as capturing or sinking as many Spanish ships as they could and take prisoners.

One of these privateers was James Bonney, whose young wife Anne took up with Rackham, who had been lavishly spending his money from the sale of the booty he had robbed or stolen. When he caught sight of Anne he spent even more, to the point where the money soon ran out. But he knew that if that happened he could lose Anne too; so he became a privateer onboard a sloop commanded by another ex-pirate, John Burgess. Their trip proved to be a great success. When Rackham returned and sold his share of the goods from the privateering expedition he was a rich man and again spent all his money on Anne.

Rogers comes into this story because Anne and Rackham lived together and carried on publicly together, so much so that complaints were made. The couple were brought before Rogers. He ordered that for their callous and lewd behaviour Anne should be stripped and whipped and that Rackham should do the whipping. For her part, Anne agreed that she would behave herself in future, give up her bad ways and return to her husband. But Anne did not in fact go back to her husband nor did she give up her wild ways. Instead she and Rackham ran off together and both became pirates. All this is based on Defoe's account in *The Pyrates*. It makes a glamorous story and at face value it probably is grossly exaggerated, but there is probably some kernel of truth to it.

While Jack Rackham and Anne Bonney were cavorting around New Providence, the rest of the people were close to starving. Food was scarce and had been since Rogers's arrival. Using his own money he resolved to send letters to merchants on the nearby island of Port Prince, part of Spanish Cuba, for provisions and especially for cattle and hogs. The plan was to encourage animals to breed on New Providence, so that the inhabitants would have their own supply of dairy products and meat.

Accordingly, he organized a voyage of three ships, the schooner the *Batchelor's Adventure*, commanded by Captain Henry White, the *Lancasters* sloop, commanded by Captain Greenaway and the sloop, the *Mary*, commanded by Captain John Auger to carry out this voyage. They set sail on 5 October 1718, and anchored at Green Key Island, about fifty miles away from New Providence.

In the lush island cove where the three ships anchored, those loyal officers and crew soon found themselves victims to pirates. Onboard the *Batchelor's Adventure* was boatswain Josiah Bunce, who came aboard the *Lancaster Sloop* with his captain to consult about their sailing times. The crews exchanged small talk, the maps were brought out as the two captains consulted, and, while Bunce waited, he asked if he could have a bottle of beer. Bottles were brought for each of the men and as Bunce began to drink he started boasting about how he could command the vessel better than anyone else. Tempers began to fray under the hot sun as Bunce became louder and more obnoxious.

Bunce's actions were decoys: within minutes the *Batchelor's Adventure* had been seized by the majority of the crew who were in on the plan. The other two vessels were also seized. Those who remained loyal to Rogers and the pardon were stripped and put on the island with almost nothing. The majority of the crews of all three vessels were in on the plot as well as Captain Auger, who had decided to join in with them. Both White and Greenaway were marooned, along with the few remaining loyal men.

Three times the pirates sailed away and three times they returned. Once when they returned they beat the naked men they had marooned as sport. Another time they returned and provided the castaways with stores including ammunition, muskets and flour so that they could survive on the island alone.

Bunce had taken charge of the three vessels, but he was no Rogers. After they had left the island for the third time, they caught sight of some ships in the harbour at Long Island, one of the Bahamas islands, and decided to attack them, thinking them nothing but cargo vessels.

Bunce had made a huge mistake; had he been more experienced he would not have attacked. The three ships turned out to be experienced Spanish privateers who opened fire on the three pirate vessels heading straight for them. Shot screeched and whined all around the deck of the *Batchelor's Adventure* as Bunce ordered the ships to attack. One shot landed close to him, splintering wood, but then another hit him, mortally wounding him. The rest of the pirates were taking a mauling at the hands of the Spanish privateers, who had by now raised their anchors and were moving their ships into positions to use their cannon. The three pirate ships managed to turn away before being totally destroyed, and several pirates jumped into the water and swam to shore.

The two sloops that Rogers had sent out some time before this to look for

Vane captured the sloop on which the mortally wounded Bunce lay. Taking it to New Providence, Rogers decided to see Bunce for himself. Climbing aboard the sloop he stood over the wounded man and began questioning him. Rogers's tone was harsh and Bunce, after all his bravado, and now mortally wounded, was no hero: he confessed everything. Rogers decided to make an example of the man and have him executed the following morning. Bunce had been one of the pirates who had taken the king's pardon and turned against it. But fate had a cruel twist in store for Rogers, because the night before Bunce was due to be executed he died of his wounds.

One positive thing had come out of it though – Rogers had learned of the marooned men. He sent a sloop to find them. The pirates of the three vessels who had attacked the Spanish privateers at Long Island had managed to get ashore, where they hid from the Spanish privateers and from the English. But Rogers had a trump card. Reformed pirate Benjamin Hornigold became Rogers's weapon against the outlaws. In a letter to his backers he outlines his impression of Hornigold: 'Having lately had intelligence of certain pirates who had run away with some vessels fitted out from this port where they might be found I equipped a sloop with sufficient men and arms under the command of Captain Hornigold and Captain Cockram who had themselves been Pirates but accepted of His Majesty's act of grace and by their behaviour since my arrival gave me full confidence of their sincerity which has been successfully confirmed by their apprehending them to the number of thirteen three whereof dyed of their wounds; I am glad of this new proof Captain Hornigold has given the world to wipe off the infamous name he has hither been known by. Though he has admitted most people spoke well of his generosity.'

Rogers was convinced Hornigold's reformation was genuine, so he sent him out in search of the pirates. Hornigold's main target was still the elusive Charles Vane. Sent by Rogers to find Vane and the marooned pirates, Hornigold was gone a long time as he cruised the islands, picked up the marooned pirates while shadowing Vane, keeping him as close as he could while waiting for the right opportunity to attack. In the meantime, Rogers, weak, exposed and vulnerable could only wait. Had Hornigold turned back to piracy? Had he joined with Vane and would he soon be sailing over the horizon to take back New Providence?

Chapter 12

Rough Justice

Fearing a revolt among the newly reformed pirates at Nassau Rogers decided to send some prisoners to England to be tried there. 'By the Ship *Samuel W Taylor* hence for England on the 11 November being the first and only opportunity I have had hence since my arrival, in that Ship I sent three men Prisoners being accused of piracy and the evidences for the King together with the allegations delivered here upon oath, whereby they appear very guilty of the accusations,' Rogers wrote in a letter to his backers and the Secretary of State for the Southern Department, James Craggs the Younger. 'I was at that time too weak to bring them to a trial for most of the people here having led the same course of life I did not know but if I had tried them after sentence brought to execution but an insurrection might have rescued them from the guard service. I did not think myself secure to try the Pirates.'

Rogers continued to worry about Hornigold. Where was he? Why was he taking so long?

Finally, Hornigold returned: having lost Vane he had decided to get the pirates who had attacked the privateers at Long Island, but they were so badly mauled by them that they had abandoned their own vessels and fled to the shore, where they hid. These men would have known Hornigold because he was a pirate himself at one point. Cruising close inshore Hornigold knew he would have to do something a little different. He sent across a man who was a complete stranger to the pirates who acted as if he was the captain of the sloop, not Hornigold. In Defoe's account of the story the man's name is not mentioned but Defoe states that he told the pirates he could provide them with food and water aboard his ship. The pirates came aboard willingly – and Hornigold had his prisoners. Their fates were sealed. Hornigold set sail for New Providence.

An example had to be made. Rogers wrote to the government in England about his intentions. 'These last prisoners were brought to me when I was made stronger and after a leisure I had to peruse and consider of my power invested by my Commission and instructions wherein I perceived the manner required of me to act concerning pirates and their accessories,' he wrote.

'As soon as the fort is finished and the guns mounted which I hope will be done before the Christmas holy days are over, I will then do the best I can to make examples of some of them by which time I hope to have more of them in Custody.'

A month after Hornigold's return Rogers began to feel safe enough to make that example. He set up a Vice-Admiral Court, where those captured pirates were put on trial. A private consultation took place in the city of Nassau on 28 November 1718 and was entered into the council records as follows:

The Governor acquainted us that Captains Cockram and Hornigold by virtue of commission had been directed to apprehend certain pirates and were successful in bringing ten of them prisoners to New Providence who were confined on the ship Delicia *and therefore desired we might agree to join in one opinion concerning the prisoners. For want of a jail, guards were set on the prisoners. As many as can be spared daily worked on the fortifications and did the guard duty at night thereby harassing our small numbers of men and hindering the public work. There are still those in these parts, who might give intelligence on the condition of our colony and should any fear be shown on our part, might motivate those already here to invite the pirates to attempt the rescue of the prisoners. We believe it is for the public good when the fort is in a better state of defence that Captain Beauchamp and Captain Burgess, with about 60 soldiers and seamen gone to prevent the designs of Vane the Pirate, return to strengthen us. As soon as possible the Governor ought then (notwithstanding he has made known to us that he has no direct commission for putting pirates on trial: yet according to the intent and meaning of the sixth article of the Governor's Instructions, which is corroborated with the power in the Governor's commission of Governor, Captain-General and Vice-Admiral of the Bahamas Islands shows the intention of His Majesty for authority here and that there is an account that government of Carolina executed 22 pirates after first accepting His Majesty's grace then turned pirates again, and considering it would be great trouble to send so many prisoners to Great Britain and even greater trouble to keep them here) we are of the opinion that His Majesty will approve of the necessity of the Governor proceeding judiciously with these pirates by a trial according to law and we believe that the speediest execution for those found guilty will conduce most to the welfare of the government.*

Rogers wrote a letter dated 8 December 1718 to council members William Fairfax, Captain Robert Beauchamp, Thomas Walker, Captain Wingate Gale, Nathaniel Taylor, Captain Josias Burgess and Captain Peter Courant outlining his plans for trying and sentencing the pirates:

> *By virtue of a commission from his most sacred Majesty King George, King of Great Britain I have the power and authority to empower and commission proper judges for the trying, determining, adjudging and condemning of all or any pirates brought into this government and in confidence of the loyalty prudence, I do authorise and appoint you deputy judges and commissioners of the said court to be set in the city of Nassau on Tuesday the 9th of this instant to examine, hear, try and judge, determine and condemn all pirates currently in custody who are brought before the court to be tried for the offences of piracy and to proceed according to the laws of England.*

The court convened on 9 and 10 December 1718 at the fort in Nassau before the council, which included Governor Woodes Rogers, William Fairfax, Judge of the Admiralty, Robert Beauchamp, Thomas Walker, Captain Wingate Gale, Nathaniel Taylor, Captain Josias Burgess and Captain Peter Courant. The Governor's commission for setting up the court was read out. The pirates were charged with mutiny, felony and piracy. A court clerk stood up to make the proclamation that all those people required or summoned to appear in the court were duly in attendance. The prisoners were then brought to the bar and called by name – John Augur, William Cunningham, John Hipps, Dennis Macarty, George Rounsivell, William Dowling, William Lewis, Thomas Morris, George Bendall and William Ling. Each man held up his hand and was identified by his name and position in the dock.

The charges were read as follows:

> *You the said John Augur, Will Cunningham, John Hipps, Dennis Macarty, George Rounsivell, William Dowling, William Lewis, Thomas Morris, George Bendall and William Ling having all of you lately received the benefit of His Majesty's most gracious pardon and having since taken the oaths of allegiance to his most sacred Majesty King George and thereupon trust has been reposed in you lawful employment been bestowed to deliver you all from your former unlawful courses of life, and to enable and support you all in just and lawful ways of living: and*

you not having the Fear of God before your eyes, nor any regard to your Oaths of Allegiance nor to the Performance of Loyalty, Truth and Justice: but being deluded by the Devil to return to your former unlawful evil courses of Robbery and Pyracy and that you did on the 6th day of the Reign of our Sovereign Lord George, by the Grace of God, King of Great Britain plot and combine together at a desolate island called, Green Key Island to mutiny and feloniously steal, take away from the Commanders and Owneres of the sloops, the Batchelor's Adventure, *the* Lancaster *and the* Mary *tackle apparel and furniture to the value of above £900 current money of these Islands and by force cause to be put ashore on the said desolate Island one Mr James Carr, merchant and sundry others with him and the said John Augur as then commander of one of the said sloops did proceed as commander of the said pirates from the said Island of Green Key Island to Exuma where directed to Captain John Cockram and Captain Benjamin Hornigold you the said John Augur and the rest of your piratical company were there taken and apprehended as pirates and thereupon brought into this port to be proceeded against according to law.*[30]

The prisoners were then asked how they pleaded, guilty or not guilty. All of them answered 'not guilty', and it was then ordered that the King's Evidence be sworn in and examined.

The first witness for the Crown was James Carr, who stood in the witness box and said under oath that being outbound from New Providence on a trading voyage in the sloop *Mary* 'in about two days sail did arrive at Green Key Island with two other vessels in company bound also on the trading account where on the 6th of October last, Phineas Bunce, one of the *Mary*'s company and the head mutineer of the pirates but since deceased did came onboard the sloop *Mary* and treated me very vilely.' Carr continued by saying that he was sent ashore on Green Key Island by the pirates, where he was treated very badly by all except Dennis Macarty, who showed them some civility.

Next for the king was the examination of Captain William Greenaway, master of the sloop *Lancaster*. He took the oath, stood at the witness stand and said that on 6 October last John Hipps, one of the prisoners at the bar, came with some others onboard his vessel with the pretensions of getting some tobacco:

He told me that Mr Carr had a mind to sail that night and I having
ordered his boat to go onboard the Schooner, to give them notice of Carr's
design; in which Interim John Augur and George Rounsivell came
aboard. James Mathews and John Johnson, wanted me to go onboard the
Schooner, which I did, where Phineas Bunce, met me at the side and I
demanded of Bunce the reason he did not prepare for sailing as the rest
did. Whereupon Bunce, the head Mutineer asked me to walk down into
the cabin and when there Bunce asked me to sit down beside him; where
he told me that I was a prisoner upon which Dennis Macarty, pointed a
pistol at my chest and told me if I spoke a word I was a dead man.

Continuing his testimony, Greenaway said that Bunce told him to be easy as most of the crew of the schooner were on his (Bunce's) side as well as the people he had brought with him. All of this took place at night, just off Green Key Island. Bunce then went aboard the *Mary* and took her.

Greenaway, locked in the cabin, was unable to tell who were the rest of the men helping Bunce. His misfortune did not end there, as he states: 'Bunce and the prisoners now at the bar, except John Hipps, put Mr James Carr, Richard Turnley, Thomas Rich, John Taylor and John Cox all ashore at Green Key Island and had the boat ready to take me ashore also.'

But Bunce intervened, Greenaway testified. He declared that Greenaway, being a Bermudian, would swim aboard again and so confined Greenaway as a prisoner aboard his own vessel, which he and the rest of the pirates then plundered, leaving him with nothing except a small quantity of flour and beef. Bunce told Greenaway not to sail away from Green Key Island for twenty-four hours after he and the rest of the pirates had left. However, Greenaway did sail the next morning for New Providence. 'And as I did I fell in sight of the mutineers and pyrates some of whom are at the bar, and they gave chase. Whereupon I went back to Green Key Island and took to the Shore.' At this point the pirates cut away the mast of the *Lancaster* and then came on shore to take him prisoner. Escaping into the interior of the desolate Green Key Island Greenaway managed to elude the pirates. He later learned from the rest of the crew and passengers left on his vessel and then sent ashore by the pirates that Bunce and his men had scuttled her.

Greenaway then testified that he had heard that the pirates had moved on from Green Key Island to Long Island where they had met the Spanish and, as we have seen, were so badly mauled in their attack on the Spanish privateers that they had to hide ashore.

Rogers listened to the testimony and watched Greenaway return to his seat. Then John Taylor came forward and took the oath. He claimed that all the prisoners except John Hipps had joined with Bunce who took the vessel which he was part of and that for a short time Hipps was a prisoner with Greenaway.

Rogers and the council listened to more King's Evidence, this time from Richard Turnley, who took the oath and said that on 6 October Bunce, along with William Dowling and Thomas Morris, boarded the sloop *Mary* at Green Key Island. According to Turnley's evidence Bunce asked Carr for a bottle of beer for each of his men, which was given to them. He then asked for another and then for a third. 'Then with the men belonging to the sloop *Mary* took up Arms and took Mr Carr, Thomas Cox and myself Prisoners and forced us to go ashore at Green Key Island, a desolate place.'

Next it was John Cox who testified for the Crown. Blinking in the light, he placed his hand on the Bible, swore the oath, then began his testimony. He said that he was aboard the sloop *Mary*, commanded by John Augur. According to Cox, Augur came onboard his sloop on the evening of 6 October and pretended to sleep. After a short time Captain Greenaway came aboard to ask Augur if he intended to set sail and Augur answered that he could not tell. Cox then says that Greenaway left the *Mary* and boarded the schooner the *Batchelor's Adventure*, where Henry White was master. About half an hour later White went onboard the sloop *Lancaster* with John Hipps to search for Greenaway.

Cox then stated that not long afterwards Bunce boarded the *Mary* with two or three men asking Captain Augur if there was anything to drink. Coming to Mr Carr, Bunce asked him for a bottle of beer. Carr gave him the beer. Cox then said that Bunce went into the cabin and brought out a cutlass, announcing he was the captain of the *Mary*, 'which made Captain Augur ask him his Meaning but presently Bunce and Augur seemed to be good friends and Bunce asked for another Bottle of Beer and struck Mr Carr with the cutlass on his back and turned him, myself and the others ashore. All the prisoners except Hipps were Aiders, Assistants and Abettors to the Mutiny, Felony and Pyracy.'

Rogers and the rest of the judges listened carefully to the next testimony as Thomas Rich swore under oath that he knew all the prisoners and that all, except Hipps, were the actors of the mutiny and piracy that was committed upon the vessels. Rich was put ashore with Carr by the pirates from the *Mary*.

Thomas Petty, also under oath, gave his deposition for the Crown, saying that he saw Bunce beat Hipps and believed that Hipps was forced to go with

Bunce. Bunce was about to force Petty to go as well but Dennis Macarty, one of the collaborators, told Bunce that if he forced Petty to go with them he would leave Bunce and his company of cutthroats.

Though it was December, the humidity in the fort was building up and Rogers adjourned the court until three o'clock that afternoon. When the court resumed each of the prisoners was called to provide their defence. First to speak was John Augur, a respected master of ships, around 40 years old, who had fallen in with the pirates and had accepted the king's pardon, then returned to pirate ways. He shuffled to the witness stand, took the oath and swore that he was drunk and did not know Phineas Bunce or his purpose 'when he came aboard the *Mary* but I have no evidence to prove I am not guilty'.

Rogers looked the man up and down. 'Come man, have you nothing to say in your defence?' This was a man whom Rogers had trusted with a good vessel and valuable cargo for an important voyage to secure food and supplies for the settlement. He must have wondered at his own lack of judgement. Rogers was from a Puritan family and could not conceive of a man breaking or betraying a trust; and yet, in front of him, was one such man. Augur knew he was guilty, Rogers knew he was guilty. Throughout the trial Auger appeared to be very penitent and neither washed, shaved or changed his old clothes, 'and when he stood on the ramparts and was given his last glass of wine wished for the success of the Bahama Islands and the Governor.'

William Cunningham's defence was that he was asleep when Bunce boarded the schooner to which Cunningham belonged. Bunce told Cunningham that he must either join him or be marooned. Around 45 years old, he acted in much the same way as Augur did, penitent to the last.

In his defence, John Hipps testified that he did not get involved with Bunce and his men but went onboard the *Batchelor's Adventure* to enquire after Captain Greenaway, his own captain, and was immediately imprisoned with Greenaway by Bunce. Later they were put on shore with Carr and the others. Once ashore, Bunce beat Hipps to force Hipps to join them. Hipps replied he would leave Bunce and company at the first opportunity. Hipps then asked that Carr, Captain Greenaway, Richard Turnley, Thomas Terrell, Benjamin Hutchins, John Taylor, John Janson, Thomas Petty and David Meredith might be called to speak for him.

Rogers nodded his head and James Carr was called forth. Carr took the oath, his testimony being sworn in as evidence for the prisoner and claimed, 'Bunce used much threatening language against John Hipps saying that if he did not join the pirates and go with them Hipps should repent the refusal.' Carr continued by saying that he did not see or know of any attacks or blows given by the pirates to Hipps to compel him to assist or join them, but that he afterwards accepted the office of command of boatswain to the pirates.

Under oath, Captain Greenaway, speaking for Hipps, said 'he boarded the Schooner with me and was in the cabin of the Schooner when we were both made prisoners and Hipps proposed to escape by surprising one of the Prisoners at the Bar Dennis Macarty and throw him overboard.'

'What did you say to that?' Rogers questioned Greenaway.

'I replied that we were unlikely to get away from the rest of the pirates so he should keep his ideas to himself until he could see a better opportunity to escape.' Greenaway then said that Hipps was put ashore with Carr and others.

Next was Richard Turnley, who corroborated Greenaway's evidence, adding that he also never saw Bunce or any other man beat Hipps to force him to join them. Also speaking for Hipps, as a character witness, was Thomas Terrell. He told the court that Hipps was an honest man and had been recommended to him by Thomas Bowling, master of the sloop *Sarah*, which belonged to Terrell. Bowling stated that on a recent voyage a mutiny took place and Bowling declared that Hipps had put down the mutiny and that the safety of the vessel was down to John Hipps.

Thomas Petty and Benjamin Hutchins both swore they had seen Hipps badly treated by Bunce and backed up some of the evidence already given, while another witness, David Meredith, said that Bunce had beaten Hipps many times until Hipps gave in and joined the pirates.

Having heard Meredith's evidence Rogers and his judges then turned to the rest of the prisoners, asking them if they knew of anyone who could speak for them. Each prisoner asked for someone to come forward and speak for them, but almost to a man the people they asked to come forward did not speak favourably. Thomas Rich, for example, gave evidence for Thomas Morris, who claimed he was drunk the whole time. Rich, on the other hand, stated that 'Morris appeared to be as active as the most capable and could not say that the Prisoner ever relented.' Similarly, Richard Turnley speaking for the prisoner William Lang, declared that Lang had borne arms and was as resolved as any of the other pirates.

There were other examples. Carr was called to speak for David Macarty but said that he was as active as any of the other men who turned to piracy. Also for Macarty the court recognized Thomas Rich, who said he had heard Macarty say that since he had begun being a pirate he thought he should stay one.

Petty came forward again, this time for Macarty. He swore he heard the young man say, 'He was sorry for his unadvisedness, which might bring great troubles on his poor wife having a small child.'

After hearing from the witnesses to speak for Macarty, Rogers turned to Rounsivell and said: 'George Rounsivell do you wish to have anyone to speak for you?'

'I beg the Court's pardon and ask that John Turnley give evidence for me,' he replied. Turnley, sworn in, said that Rounsivell, even though he consented to be one of Bunce's men, had some sorrow for what he was doing but on danger of his life could not desert the pirates he had started with.

Rogers listened to the testimony. He had trusted all the men before him to go out to secure the supplies the little settlement badly needed to keep going. They had all taken the king's pardon and now they stood before him as having betrayed the trust. With the evidence heard on both sides, Rogers then adjourned the court until ten o'clock the next day.

Accordingly at ten on the morning of 10 December 1718 the court reconvened. As the prisoners were brought in Rogers stared at them. 'Do you have anything further to say in your defence?' he asked. None of them did. The court then asked if there was anyone who had anything to say favourably about Hipps. At that moment, the dusty doors opened and the constable, Samuel Lawford, entered the court and moved up to the witness stand, all eyes following him. Swearing on oath he said, 'I heard George Redding say that he should have been glad to have done the old Boatswain any service, meaning Hipps. For Redding had seen him cry for his having consented tho' by force to join Bunce & co.'

'What else did he say?'

'The Prisoner also declared to me that he would fight each of the pirates singly if he could get clear of them. I firmly believe that the Prisoner would have escaped from the other pirates as soon as he could have got an opportunity.'

Again the prisoners were asked if they had anything further to add. The reply was 'no', except for Dennis Macarty, who finally made a wise decision and asked that Captain Benjamin Hornigold should speak for him. The captain said under oath that 'when I went to apprehend the prisoners Macarty was one of the first taken and seemed to me to throw himself and to have dependence on the mercy of the Governor.'

Prisoner William Lewis asked that Richard Turnley be recalled to speak in his defence. Turnley strode to the witness stand, where he was sworn in and asked if he had anything else he could add in Lewis's defence. He said: 'I did not see the prisoner when the sloop *Mary* was first taken but the day after I saw the Prisoner under arms as active as any one of the pirates.'

George Bendall, the ninth prisoner, asked Carr to be recalled to speak for him. Under oath Carr declared that 'I heard the prisoner say that he wished he'd begun the life sooner for he thought it a pleasant one, that is the life of a pirate. He also said that he had a strong inclination to have smothered John Graves Esq his Majesty's Collector for the Islands as he lay ill and weak in his bed for the prisoner was for a short time a servant of Mr Graves before he shipped himself for the intended voyage and joined the other prisoners in their mutiny and piracy.'

With this now done, the prisoners were remanded to the fort while the court began their deliberations. All the prisoners except John Hipps were unanimously voted guilty and ordered to be sentenced. Hipps was remanded into custody and his judgement delayed. He was sent in irons to the guardship *Delicia* while the rest of the prisoners were brought in again.

'Do any of you know any cause why sentence of death should not be pronounced upon you?' Rogers asked. There was a shuffling of feet, a cough and many of the prisoners shook their heads. But they said nothing.

The clerk of the court then read out the sentence:

> *The Court having duly considered of the evidence which hath been given against you the said John Augur, William Cunningham, Dennis Macarty, George Rounsivell, William Dowling, William Lewis, Thomas Morris, George Bendall and William Ling and having debated the several circumstances of the cases it is adjudged that you are guilty of the mutiny, felony and piracy. And the Court doth accordingly pass sentence that you be carried from whence you came and from thence to the place of execution where you are to be hanged by the neck till you shall be dead; and God have mercy on your souls.*

Rogers, as governor and President of the Court, then set their execution at ten o'clock on the following Friday, 12 December 1718. Before being sent out of the court, they were allowed to pray for a long time to prepare for death.

Rogers had the last word and spoke to the prisoners. He said that from the time they had been caught on 15 November they should have seen themselves as having been condemned by the laws of all nations, and their fate was now sealed. He continued by saying that the time taken in securing them for the court and the favour that the court had allowed them to make so long a defence had taken up all the time they had. Looking at each of the prisoners in turn, he paused. 'I have been obliged to employ all my people to assist in mounting the great guns and in finishing the present Works with all possible Dispatch, because of the expected war with Spain and there being many more Pyrates amongst these Islands, and this Place left destitute of all Relief from any Man of War or Station Ships I am indispensably obliged for the welfare of this settlement to give you no more Time.' He then ordered that the prisoners be taken back to their place of imprisonment in the fort where they were given leave to send for any persons to read and pray with them.

Before ten on the morning of the execution, the Provost-Marshal, Thomas Robinson Esquire, commissioned to the role for the day, had the prisoners released from their irons, pinioned them and then ordered the guards to assist him in leading them to the top of the ramparts facing the sea.

That morning the prisoners had an audience, for more than a hundred soldiers and civilians had gathered at the ramparts to watch the event. The prisoners had requested that prayers and psalms be read, which was done, with everybody joining in. After the last hymn died away, Robinson was ordered to conduct the prisoners down a ladder to the foot of a wall where the gallows had been erected. A black flag fluttered in the warm morning breeze.

Dennis Macarty wore long blue ribbons around his neck, wrists, knees and cap, and once on the ramparts looked around cheerfully. 'I knew the time when there were many brave Fellows on the Island who would not have suffered me to die like a dog,' he said. With that he flung off both his shoes and kicked them over the parapet. 'I promised not to die with my shoes on.'

Another young man, William Dowling, aged 24, had been with the pirates a long time and even after accepting the king's pardon never reformed. Another prisoner, 34-year-old William Lewis, had been a prize fighter before turning pirate. He appeared to be completely unconcerned by his impending death and was interested only in getting as drunk as he could while everyone looked on. One of the youngest men, 22-year-old Thomas Morris, showed no remorse whatsoever. As he climbed up to the stage he declared: 'We have a new Governor and a Harsh one.' Like Macarty he wore ribbons all over him, red instead of the blue. As he stood there on the stage he was heard to say, 'I might have been a greater Plague to these Islands and I now wish I had been.' The youngest man there, George Bendall, was only 18 but was totally unrepentant. Sullen and moody, 'he had all the villainous Inclinations that the most profligate youth could be infected with.'[31] Finally, William Ling, aged 30, behaved in a truly penitent manner and was not heard to say anything other than by reply when Lewis demanded wine to drink: Ling said that water was more suitable at that time. In all, 'There were few except for the Governor's people who had not deserved the same fate among the spectators but for the fact they had taken the King's Act of Grace [pardon].'

Under the gallows was a stage supported by three butts that the prisoners reached by going up another ladder. It was here that the hangman waited. He fastened the cords around the necks of each of the prisoners with quick dexterity. For the next three-quarters of an hour more psalms and hymns were sung while the spectators edged as close as they could to the foot of the gallows until pushed back by the marshal's guards.

As the morning breeze coming across the harbour gently ruffled the clothes of the onlookers Rogers made a sudden decision. 'Free George Rounsivell,' he said to the captain of the guard. There were gasps from the crowd. Rogers heard the young man came from good Dorset stock, his parents living in Weymouth. He ordered Rounsivell to be unbound and put under guard until he was eventually pardoned.

Did Rogers wait to free the man at the last minute because he suddenly discovered his background or was it because he wanted to make a spectacle to create maximum impact? He may have thought that showing the crowds he could be merciful as well as harsh might have a profound effect on the colony.

The remaining eight prisoners, though fully unrepentant, must have wondered if they too might be pardoned. They were not. Suddenly, the trestles were kicked away by the executioner and one by one the eight men dropped, the ropes biting into each neck, snapping them like twigs. Their bodies twitched at the end of the ropes as they died in the morning sun to the shocked silence of the crowd. But this form of rough justice, meted out by Rogers, had a powerful impact and in effect brought piracy in New Providence to an end.

Tired, hot and worn out, Rogers trudged back to his house. In the letter he wrote to England the following day he laid out his reasons for sparing George Rounsivell. 'This is a desire to respite him for his future repentance, till I know His Majesty's Pleasure. He is the son of loyal and good parents at Weymouth in Dorset. And since His Majesty has been so graciously pleased to be so extensive in his acts of pardon to the pirates; I hope this unhappy young man will deserve his life and I beg the honour of your intercession with His Majesty for me in his behalf.'

As 1718 drew to a close we can see how Rogers was feeling. 'I would not undergo the like fatigue and rigour I have done ever since I have been here for the profits of any employment on earth but I hope I am now out of danger at least of Pirates.' Vane would never return, the little settlement was free to get on with the business of rebuilding and restarting its trade. By Christmas Eve 1718, when Rogers wrote to Secretary Craggs in London, things were starting to get a little better.

Chapter 13

Spain Attacks

'The people here are very lazy and poor and provisions scarce so that I cannot subsist the garrison at the rate it was undertaken last year. I have been already forced to drain several bills that supported me to begin this settlement and if I have till March I design to send by an officer hence an account of the whole experience of this colony that his majesty and those gentlemen may be rightly apprised of the difficulty of their undertaking for I hope these honourable gentlemen will not suffer by venturing to serve the public with so little assistance at a juncture when the attempt was and is so very precarious and cannot for some time be of any advantage but to the public.'

Woodes Rogers

The threat of a Spanish attack still remained uppermost in his mind. Prior to his writing to Secretary Craggs, Rogers had heard of the destruction of more than half of Spain's fine new fleet off Cape Passaro at the southern end of Sicily by Sir George Byng. Official hostilities in the form of the War of the Quadruple Alliance followed, where Austria, France, the Netherlands and England went to war against Spain.

Spanish ambitions were driven by two Italians, Queen Elizabeth Farnese, second wife of Philip V, and Cardinal Giulio Alberoni, more of a politician than a holy man. The queen was anxious to gain as much for Italy as for her son, the future King Charles III, while King Philip V of Spain ordered his viceroys and governors to retake all the settlements and colonies in the Americas that had belonged to Spain. Even those places where Spain had made a claim but actually had no presence Philip ordered retaken. That included the Bahamas. With Havana so close, Rogers knew that it would not be long before Spanish ships appeared. In the meantime, the main objectives for the Spaniards were Florida, which they still held, the Carolinas and Louisiana.

As 1719 dawned, Rogers's anxiety increased. The fortifications on New Providence were nowhere near capable of mounting a defence against a determined attack. No help was forthcoming from the British Government. Rogers's sending of letter after letter asking for more soldiers, for a warship to visit for protection, had resulted only in silence. We know the letters got through because they are kept in the National Archives at Kew, so one has to wonder what the Crown was doing. Why did they not respond? Were they so badly stretched there was nothing they could do and no resources available for them to do anything? Why was Rogers not told? Whatever the answer, Rogers was left to his own devices, to keep the colony going at his own expense and use whatever local resources he had to improve the defences.

He gathered intelligence wherever he could. An entry in the council records dated 12 January 1719 illustrates the desperate straits they were in and how much they depended on mere scraps of information:

> *The Governor made known to the council that a French sloop lately arrived here from St Thomas with advice from the Governor thereof that the Spaniards were now in readiness and had taken resolutions to attempt this settlement, which this sloop had met another sloop of this port which, told them that our fort and garrison were in a tollerable posture of defence but provisions wanted, which incited this French sloop aforementioned to bring Certain provisions for the life and safeguard of our garrison and Island. Therefore, the Governor desired the opinon of the council how far they judged the necessity of our affairs might justify the Governor's buying the necessary provision although our laws prohibit any goods coming into this settlement from foreign vessels.*
>
> *The council having well considered the reasons of the said French sloop coming into this port and the provisions therein brought, may be of great service for this Settlement.*

Early in the New Year Rogers uncovered a plot among some of the more immoral people of the settlement to kill him and his officers and hand the island back to the pirates. In a letter dated 24 January 1719 he talks about this plot:

> *On 27 October [1718] I had a letter from Commodore Chamberlain dated 20th October in his passage from New York he had then a fair wind to come here but 30 leagues hence. But thought fit to pass me with a compliment without giving me hope of seeing him or either of the two that with us here, and as I am well informed more bound for Petty Guanay and hence to Jamaica whither immediately dispatched an express to the Governor of Jamaica and him for assistance, the ship of War disregard this settlement may like to prove of a very ill consequence by encouraging*

the loose people and some of my own sailors, palatines and French who came to me they privately conduct to leave the settlement, some ring leaders had secretly agreed to seize or destroy me and my officers and then to deliver up the fort to the hands of the pirates. I having timely notice of it secured three of the principals and punished them with a severe whipping but cannot spare them send them hence, I shall release them and be more on my guard.

Should he have mounted another mass hanging? He had to be careful how he acted, showing leniency as well as swift justice. It is interesting to note here that less than a month after the mass hanging of pirates Rogers felt he had no power to try and convict the three ringleaders of this plot. Surely it was treason. Perhaps his real fear was that his power was so precarious that by staging another hanging he would have an uprising.

Knowing that these enemies were still among the people of the settlement, he pressed ahead with the fortifications, moving backwards and forwards between the forts and the houses, desperate to ensure that they had some form of defence.

Disease was still rife in the colony. The inhabitants were lazy, drunk most of the time and hated any kind of hard work. Only once did Rogers manage to get them to work hard and that was for two weeks after he had doled out free food and drink, playing on the fear of a Spanish invasion. 'The people did for fourteen days work vigorously, seldom less than two hundred men a day, but nothing but their innate thirst of revenge on the Spaniards could prompt them to such zeal which was so strong that they forgot they were at the same time strengthening a curb for themselves,' Rogers wrote in his letter of 24 January 1719. This petered out and the main body of inhabitants went back to their old ways, spending their time in the taverns and drinking houses rather than worrying about keeping their newly built houses and their families safe and secure.

Rogers could only rely on a handful of people, his officers and soldiers, those who were fit enough and the black slaves, to keep working to rebuild the island's fortifications. 'The advice of the preparation of the Spaniards to attack this place I have received on the sixth of February has kept me continually employed to provide for their reception, has made me write letters to all parts around us for assistance but none of His Majesty's ships being near us,' Rogers wrote. 'I fear they'll scarce be here time enough to help defend this place for which reason I spare no time, nor cost to secure this place. Expenses we have been at to support this colony which we hope to do against the Spaniards. I have heard nothing of the pirates since my foregoing letter and I hope they have took their course another way or that justice has met with them.'

In London, Rogers's backers and partners had up to this point spent £11,394 on keeping the *Delicia* anchored in Nassau harbour and on the fortifications. Deeply in debt, Rogers's main worry was the lack of any capital and his rapidly exhausting credit.

On 19 February 1719 at a council meeting held at Rogers's house it was decided that an embargo, which the council had set up some weeks before, had come to its expiration date and needed to be reinstated. 'Not having any account of the disposition of the Spanish Ships and sloops of War ready to sail from the Havana since the late intelligence raised and the reasons being as necessary for continuing the embargo as at first wherefore the Governor and council thought it convenient for the safety of this government be ordered that the embargo be not taken off.' At that same meeting the council agreed that Captain Thomas Fornier, commander of a French ship that had been brought in by one of the privateers Rogers had sent out to harass the Spanish, should sail back for France so that his cargo of sugar would not spoil.

The council then heard a disposition from Captain Hildesley,[32] which was entered into the records. This was an answer to a letter the council had sent to him asking him for help in defending the little colony. This was his reply: 'Having lately received your letter desiring my assistance in the defence of this government which I understand is in danger of being invaded by the enemy from the Havana, I send this to assure you that nothing shall be wanting in me towards your defence in case the enemy should land or attempt it.' But, as the entry in the council records of New Providence states, Hildesley was also being asked by the government of South Carolina to come to their assistance as well. 'As I have very pressing letters from the government of South Carolina setting forth the great danger they are in of being attacked from St Augustine and the distracted condition the inhabitants are in at present having already disposed their lawfull governor from his government, will make me in a little time turn my thoughts towards the support of them likewise, however I will stay here so long as you shall apprehend any danger from the present expected invasion. I am Your most humble servant Captain Hildesley.'

In a council meeting of March 1719 an entry was placed in the records that read out the declaration of war with Spain. 'Captain Philip Cockran arriving on the 16th of this month from Barbadoes brought His Majesty's declaration of war against Spain which was immediately read and proclaimed. Whereupon several petitions were presented by several commanders of port sloops praying his Excellency's commission to fit and man the vessels to begin their first attack on the Spaniard.' According to this entry, Rogers considered the petitions and also the information fromThomas Walker, who had returned from Havana, reporting that the Spanish had several English prisoners and were treating them badly. Walker had demanded the release of the prisoners from the Spanish governor and was refused, barely escaping with his own life. Rogers decided to take as many Spaniards as he could in exchange for the prisoners being held. He commissioned five well-manned and well-armed vessels to set sail for the Spanish Reaches of the Florida coast for the express purpose of taking and surprising Spanish vessels working those waters. Council notes state that 'the effecting of which, promising so great advantage to this Settlement as well as weakening such a part of the enemy as live by sea employment. The Governor gave immediate encouragement to such commanders and men as would adventure to do the services aforesaid.' Rogers made it known to the council he hoped the vessels would bring back as much intelligence as they could on the Spanish ambitions to attack them as well as bringing back Spanish prisoners and even much needed supplies.

At another council meeting held at the fort of Nassau, Thursday, 7 May 1719 with Rogers, James Galier, Robert Beauchamp, William Fairfax, Thomas Walker, Wingate Gale and Matthew Taylor present, they were told about Captain George Hooper, who had brought in two sloops with him and 'no fewer than five prisoners for which provisions should be made for their subsistence'. The council met on summons and debated about the most merciful method to take such care as is customary: 'It was thereupon resolved that Mr Golier being desired by the council to advance such provisions for the sentences of the prisoners as might support them whilst at work on the fortifications till His Majesty's pleasure should be known concerning the relief of such prisoners that might be brought to the islands during the present war with Spain. Mr Golier agreed.'

In a letter to Secretary Craggs dated 17 May 1719 Rogers poured out his frustration:

> *I wrote you by two conveyances since I had the honour of yours by the* Deal Castle *and the* Samuel *of the 24th of December last. The* Samuel Taylor *has stayed here longer than we expected and would have continued yet a few days had not the* Endosa Acco, *came to my hands of yesterday by chance. I may expect to be soon attacked and am preparing to make the best defence I can. I doubt I shall scarce be able to get together*

above 300 men. Were we but 200 more being well prepared I should not be under any great concern for this Spanish expedition.

I have always been as particular as I could towards you and have represented everything to the best of my knowledge and I am sorry His Majesty's ships of war in these parts have had so little regard for this infant coloney. We have had none but the Deal Castle *as a packet ever since the first of our arrival, those I wrote to Jamaica and all parts around asking for assistance when we had great reason to expect we should not be able to withstand an enemy, but the Spaniards, loosing three of their best ships destined for this place, and hearing the news of war immediately upon it, made them then disperse 3 or 400 men they had ready at several places to joyne and attack us.*

I have been at great expense to prepare this place from the Spaniards or the pirates, an account of which has now been sent home to the gentlemen concerned, and I hope His Majesty will consider the necessity I was under to do all I have done and that Parliament will reimburse what is apparently paid out for the publick good.

On 26 May at another council meeting, this time held at Rogers's house with Rogers, James Golier, Robert Beauchamp, William Fairfax, Thomas Walker, Edward Holmes, Nathaniel Taylor and Thomas Barnett present, they discussed the arrival of Captain Gurrant's sloop, a privateer, arriving back into Nassau harbour with intelligence from Cuba. 'Charles the son of the Thomas Walker who had escaped thence in a dree, hearing at the Havana, the Spaniards had mustered 1000 men and expected 500 more to join them from Trinidad with design to come and attack New Providence with two galleys, two brigantines and nine sloops. . . . Therefore the Governor and council were willing to provide against such an invasion, did bestow to lay a general embargo on all vessels except the sloop *Samuel Taylor* which was bound for England with the King's packet, who had dispatches and entreaties for additional soldiers and other stores necessary for the future support of this settlement.' It was agreed at this council meeting that Robert Beauchamp[33] would stay on to help train the soldiers in military discipline as well as that Captain Thompson, who was on Harbour Island, be commanded to provide assistance for the upcoming invasion.

The fighting soon began to filter to New Providence. Captain William South, commanding the sloop *Endeavour* out of New Providence, was one of the first to see action. Sailing off Porto Maria on the coast of Cuba in the company of the *Dupont* he saw another sloop out to sea, which the *Dupont* chased. Coming up to the sloop the master of the *Dupont* hailed her in English. They fired both their large cannon and all the rest of their small arms at the *Dupont*, which immediately returned their volleys. 'But perceiving the other sloop English built and English men onboard her the *Dupont* called to them asking for what reason she fired upon them being all English,' South wrote in his report. 'The sloop fired another volley then coming nearer they bid the *Dupont* lower his main sail, which he accordingly did, yet kept firing then sent their Dree aboard and entering the *Dupont*'s vessel pretended they took her for a Spaniard.'

This strange sloop was a commissioned privateer from the Jamaican government, another British colony, and was commanded by Leigh Ashworth who, after wounding seven of the *Dupont*'s crew, did his best to make amends. 'However, the two sloops stood to sea and came off the Havana where the *Dupont* took Charles son of Thomas Walker Esq of New Providence, who had been a prisoner of the Havana and just made his escape in a canoe, with two more young fellows to bring intelligence that the Spaniards have already fitted for sea, two galleys, two brigantines and seven sloops onboard of which were fifteen hundred men to dislodge the English from their settlement because they think them too near as neighbours,' South continued in his report. On hearing this intelligence the captain of the *Dupont* proceeded to sail back to New Providence but Leigh Ashworth decided he did not want to sail to New Providence. 'He swore he would have Charles Walker as his pilot and accordingly sent his dree with threats that if Charles Walker did not go freely he would haul his sloop along side of the *Dupont*'s vessels and take them out by Force, whereby Walker was forced to submit. Afterwards the *Dupont* made the best of his way for this port and further sailed not,' according to William South's deposition of the events.

In 1719 Pensacola, the main Spanish fort on the coast of western Florida, had been the scene of harsh fighting between the French and the Spanish. The French had taken it and the Spaniards fought hard to regain it, which they did. The French attacked again and the Spaniards lost it. They continued to fight up and down the Gulf coast, which gave Rogers the breathing space he so badly needed.

According to Rogers's own reports sent to England he had gained intelligence from prisoners held in Havana who had escaped and made their way to New Providence. Rogers had sloops out looking for Spanish privateers but mostly to gather as much intelligence as they could on the enemy's intentions. He knew that the Spanish in Havana had many light warships and raw troops, far superior to the numbers that he could muster. He also knew that the two largest warships the Spanish had, the *Principe* and the *Hercules*,[34] had keels that were too deep to operate in the waters around New Providence.

By February 1720 the war in Europe was dying out, but the Spanish in Cuba were still unware of this. Commanded by Don Francisco Cornejo in the frigate *S. Josef*, a flotilla of Spanish vessels that included three smaller warships and eight sloops with more than 1,300 troops moved against the meagre 500 infantry and local militia that Rogers had at his disposal. His main protection was the *Delicia*, which was still in the harbour, and the *Flamborough*, a twenty-four gun sloop commanded by Captain Hildesley.

According to the captain's log from HMS *Flamborough* the Spanish flotilla anchored off the main entrance to Nassau harbour because Cornejo was unwilling to make a direct assault. Instead, he ordered the sloops to cruise off Hog Island, one of the islands closest to New Providence, and they stopped by the dangerous waters of the Eastern Passage. Now Cornejo had both entrances and exits covered.

On the night of the 25th the attack began as the Spanish detached a force heading for the shores of New Providence. The invasion was under way. Quietly and silently they rowed towards the shore, thinking themselves unobserved. Steadily, the shoreline beckoned. The soldiers in the landing craft made ready, fixing bayonets to their muskets, ensuring for yet one last time that their powder was dry. Officers checked their swords and their pistols. Slowly the boats neared the shore.

Suddenly the quiet of the night was broken by the sound of gunfire. Bullets ripped through the air and whizzed passed the little boats. Musket balls hammered into the wooden hulls of the boats, sending splinters flying in all directions while a cannonball landed only feet away from the lead boat.

Above the Spaniards on the little redoubt two black sentries who had seen the vessels approaching now began blazing away at them as they fell within the range of their muskets and cannon. Their fire sent alarm through the oncoming attackers and the raw untried troops fell into confusion as musket balls hacked large splinters out of their boats. Turning, they rowed hard to get out of range, unsure of the force they were facing but convinced it was a large one – that at least would have been their excuse as they rowed madly away from the continuing fire of the sentries above them.

Another Spanish force from Cuba tried to land to the west of Nassau, but was driven back by the experienced ex-pirates, now militiamen. So the great fear of a Spanish invasion had come to pass, but had been roundly defeated.

Fearing a second try Rogers decided to take no chances and continued making plans to defend his islands. For some weeks after this attempt Spanish forces remained in the waters around the Bahamas, presumably trying to mount a blockade of some description. Neither side had any idea that the war was over.

A council meeting held at Rogers's house on 3 March 1720 gives us a glimpse into the workings of the little settlement that was still hanging on by its fingernails. From an entry in the council records we can see that their primary interest at this difficult time was staying safe:

> *The Spaniards having come on the 24th within according to our late intelligence and making several attempts to land, particularly to the eastward of Mr Walker's point on which we have kept a good guard and had six guns mounted, and it being observed that such a watch has greatly disappointed the apparent designs of the enemy and that if a tower of stone was erected at said point capable to mount eight guns it would require a less number of men to keep that guard and be of greater strength to annoy any enemy that might approach it.*
>
> *Whereupon it was debated concluded and ordered that the Spanish prisoners, and such negroes as can be spared be employed in burning lime and that each white person do give his six days labour towards the said work.*

Rogers confiscated sails and rudders of small craft from those people he felt might easily turn against him and desert to the Spanish or, worse, to the pirates. Charles Vane was still at large, out there somewhere. He pressed his backers' agent Samuel Buck to put guns onto Hog Island and more in Nassau itself, and his relations with Captain Hildesley were at an all-time low. He had difficulty persuading the captain to remain until they had more reassuring news.

So at a council meeting held on 6 March it was agreed that the following morning all the council members would meet at the rise by the house of Benjamin Bullocks east of the town to reconnoitre the land opposite the house as being a good spot for constructing another tower in case they should be overrun by the Spanish or returning pirates.

A few days later the council agreed that no person should fire off their muskets or pistols. 'With that notwithstanding which many disorderly people have fired several shot amongst the shipping and vessels in the harbour also amongst the houses to the hazard of killing and wounding of people unawares especially in the time of alarm,' the entry for Tuesday, 15 March 1720 in the council records states. This meeting, like so many others, took place at the governor's house, and the following were present: Governor Woodes Rogers, James Golier, William Fairfax, Thomas Walker, Wingate Gale, Richard Thompson, Nate Taylor, Thomas Burnett and Samuel Watkins. The council ordered that anyone who fired his weapon without the permission of an officer would face a fine or imprisonment 'as the governor shall think the person culpable deserves'. The council then passed another order pertaining to anyone damaging anything: it ordered 'also that whosoever shall be convicted of destroying any thing growing in the plantations stealing or conveying away any hogs poultry or other kind of subsistence do suffer such fine or punishment as the Governor judges such person ought to have during this present alarm.'

This was a more extraordinary council meeting than most others and shows people's alarm and fear at that time. The Spanish, they felt, would surely try again; and so, to ensure they were safe, they needed as much intelligence as they could get. In the meantime, the defences needed to be as good as they could be. But a petition by the owners and masters of the sloops and other vessels tells a different story, with these men being more concerned for their livelihood than for the safety of the colony. The petition entered into the council records states: 'Whereas Captain John Hildesley has ordered our sloops and other vessels both to the eastward and westward of the fort in a direct line with the intention to stop the enemy entrance and prevent their attacking the fort and the shipping either way. . . . Wherefore we do with all submission assertain judgement that by the aforesaid posture for the vessels the shipping may be more endangered by all our sloops being set on fire and cut loose by the enemy for in such case they would fall upon our ships whilst they lie so directly in the way of the action between an approaching enemy and the cannon of His Majesty's garrison and ships the *Delicia* and French Ships.' The council then resolved that each sailor be put into possession of his own sloop.

But they were lacking in intelligence. What was the enemy up to, what were the Spanish planning? To find out Rogers directed the council to appoint Captain Seymour to cruise about the islands with his privateer sloop 'to find what intelligence he can of the enemy who have been now about twenty days gone'. The council then agreed that the embargo should be continued another eight days unless Seymour returned with news that the threat of invasion was gone or had died away for the time being.

The following day, Wednesday, 7 March 1720, the council transferred their meeting to the *Delicia* because tensions were beginning to rise between Captain Hildesley and Woodes Rogers. The records show that the dispute between the two men was referred to the council. 'Upon the result of the order of yesterday's council the masters of the vessels and boats in the harbour making after and to take their said vessels into their open possession and custody, Captain Hildesley of His Majesty's ship *Flamborough* by his office and boat obliged his vessels to continue in such pastime as he had put them, and it being disputed by the Governor and Captain Hildesley who had the command of the harbour and vessels therein and being referred to the judgment and sentiments of the council.'

The debate raged and was concluded by the council agreeing that Rogers by his commission as governor was the captain general and vice-admiral in command of the harbour and the vessels in it. 'And that Captain Hildesley had only the command onboard of His Majesty's ship *Flamborough* and of the officers and company belonging thereto and therefore in the opinion of this board that the respective masters may take their said vessels and place them according to the Governor's order.'

Furious, Hildesley agreed under oath but also said that if he got Rogers onboard he would throw him over the side. To make matters better the council came aboard with Rogers. 'The government come onboards this day to appease some tumults being collated by Captain Hildesley which matter being voluntarily referred to the council.'

The arguments went back and forth. Finally the council agreed that the colony needed Hildesley's ship and crew to remain safe. 'Especially till we can have some account of the enemy being gone the necessity of our affairs require even the greatest insults to be as moderately handed as the security and honour of the government can dispense with,' the entry in the council record books states. 'Therefore the council were of the opinion that Captain Hildesley ought to give security for his future behaviour.' Hildesley replied that since the governor and the council had given orders to the masters of the sloops to take their ships away from his command he had no other choice but to comply, but swore he would give orders as he saw fit if the enemy approached again. According to council records: 'And as to the charge of taking the Governor by the collar Captain Hildesley declared that he had no other desire than to prevent the Governor putting him under confinement as the Governor had done to the lieutenant of His Majesty's ship the master and other officers.'

Hildesley then gave his word and honour that he would act with good behaviour for the government while he remained:

To the utmost of his power together with his officers and seamen belonging to His Majesty's ship would aid and assist this government now

threatened with danger and farther added that he was ready to sign any
bond for his future good behaviour with any penalty Governor Rogers
should desire as far as five hundred or a thousand pounds.

Upon which the Governor replied that as he did not know how soon
the enemy might return with a greater force he desired all disputes might
end here and that he would take no bond for Captain Hildesley's
behaviour in hopes he should have no further cause to complain of
Captain Hildesley's conduct.

Four days later, the council met again, with the same members, debating the
fact that no assistance had come from Harbour Island despite the orders from
Rogers that it should do so. 'The Governor and council met to consider and
debate whether those two islands are of importance enough to allure any people
to settle them whilst we want inhabitants to settle and guard this island of New
Providence being the seat of Government,' ran the entry for that session in the
council records. 'Resolved and ordered that every person be obliged to come
down and do duty here from Harbour Island and Hathera Island excepting that
men to take care of the families and keep watch on each island and the seven
old persons on Harbour Island the two or three aged men on Hathera incapable
through infirmity to do duty and those who have leave today are to take their
chance by lot.'

The debate then turned to those people who had incurred debts during the
emergency, which needed to be paid. This could only be done through the
Court of Common Pleas, which the council ordered should be set up the
following week now that the enemy was nowhere to be seen.

Commodore Chamberlain had been relieved of his Jamaica command in
early 1719 by Commodore Edward Vernon, a vast improvement on
Chamberlain. He was much more willing to cooperate with the local governors,
and soon after the attempted invasion Rogers and Hildesley sent a sloop to
Vernon with the news it had been repulsed, asking him to blockade Havana.
This letter was entered into the council records on 5 April 1720 during a
council meeting at the governor's house. The council agreed to send the letter
to Commodore Vernon. 'It was with great satisfaction that we received by the
return of our vessel your letter of the 2nd of March giving us the assurance of
intent to prevent the enemy's invading us supposing at that time that you
should be early enough off the Havana to stop their proceeding.' From letters
Rogers had received from an agent of the Bahamas Company named Farril it
seems their fears were justified, since a small force had attempted to land again

but, weak from lack of water, abandoned the attempt. This information came from prisoners the Spanish had taken and then set free. 'The Spaniards gave some [prisoners] to Havana and Porto Principe,' the letter continued. 'The Commodore, with two ships, before he left these islands declared that he would suddenly return with greater force having the King of Spain's positive orders to destroy this settlement.'

In the letter to Vernon, the council stated they had continued the embargo until further advice was received. Dispatching two vessels to meet Vernon they hoped he had not sailed before they arrived:

> *Captain Hildesley is most impatient to be gone to Carolina and we have account that there is a pirate ship off Virginia for she lately took an English ship when after she had plundered gave liberty to gain. They are said to be about an hundred men and thought to be some of those come from off the coast of Guinea.*
>
> *We have prevailed with the commander of the Bermuda sloop to carry this letter together with Captain Carnegie and hope your honour will be pleased to order one of His Majesty's ships here for a few weeks seeing we cannot have Captain Hildesley longer, which service will much relieve our poor inhabitants who want, and improve the season for salt and look after their plantations. But we cannot give them leave or the merchant vessels to sail till we have a ship of war to protect us.*

Vernon, commanding the 64-gun *Mary* set sail immediately after receiving this letter and arrived off Havana where he began a blockade of the city.

A few days later, Captain Benjamin White, one of the privateers from New Providence, arrived back in Nassau with a letter from Commodore Vernon whom he had left off Cape Corrientes. He reported that he had taken two priests who had just come out of Havana with a vessel bound for Porto Principe. 'We should be much obliged if you would dispatch this vessel to us not doubting but you have had later intelligence that may import us for the trading people that are embargoed seem impatient for their enlargement and our provisions will soon become scarce. Whilst the enemy were on the blockage we found means to convey two small sloops hence for Jamaica where the Governor, in a very pressing manner desired you would please to appoint one ship of war to strengthen us and we hope if those letters did not reach you, then this may have some influence on knowledge of our necessity have thought it advisable to follow you for instructions.'

The council met again on 11 April 1720, when they debated the news received from prisoners who had escaped from Havana. 'They gave us intelligence that the enemy who were lately on our coast and returned to the Havana are now again refitting with greater force for a second expedition designed against us or Carolina and they believe will sail in ten days from the date of their letter when was the 4th of this instant, therefore the council met to consider of what proper measures ought to be taken in our present circumstances.' They decided that another ship should be sent to Commodore Vernon who had sailed for Havana as soon as he had received their first letter. That vessel carried a copy of the letter from the agent Mr Farril, and the council ordered that Captain Seymour should be the person employed for this vital service. But they had no ship available to go to South Carolina.

On 20 April, as the sun was rising, two Spanish warships, the *Principe* and the *Hercules* came out of the harbour at Havana to face Vernon's small fleet. As they drew closer the Spanish opened fire and for a short time both sides faced each other, firing volley after volley. But in the end the battle was a draw. Each side had suffered casualties and much damage. This action had the desired effect. Both sides knew the war was over and the second attack on the Bahamas never came. But by 30 April security was still a major issue for the council and for Rogers in particular. They met that day at his house to debate the situation. Captain Hildesley, who had been sent to speak with Vernon, had now returned without having met him or having had any account of the enemy. The council resolved that the minutes from the previous council meeting should be sent to Hildesley along with a letter asking him to stay longer. 'Herewith we send you a copy of the minutes of our last council and have considered that your sloop has returned but without any advice that assures our safety,' the chief clerk recorded.

'As we are promised intelligence very soon by the small vessel that waits with Seymour for that purpose so we have judged to continue the embargo and hope you will stay with us so long as we have such just reasons to desire it.' Rogers had sent another privateer captain to Cuba to get word of the Spanish intent so they could lift the embargo and begin to trade again.

The council met again on 2 May at the governor's house; present at this meeting were Woodes Rogers, James Golier, William Fairfax, Thomas Walker, Richard Thompson, Edward Holmes and Nat Taylor. The aim was to enter into the council records a letter from Captain Hildesley on the *Flamborough* that had already sailed from Nassau and that was sent directly to Rogers rather than the council. 'As you cannot expect to be in a better posture of defence than you are at present by the great number of people that are now in the place and the preparations that you have made, so you must agree that your safety is not to be doubted by the men of war being off the Havana, the sloop I sent meeting with the happy Captain Chamberlain assures me there is nothing to be feared from thence, but in case you should apprehend any further danger you may easily make your case known to Captain Vernon who has three ships under his command and will, if he finds there is any reason for it, undoubtedly send one of them to your assistance. I am well assured I have obeyd my orders and in so doing I have discharged my duty to King and Country.'

Following Hildesley's advice a letter to Commodore Vernon from Rogers and the council dated 15 May 1720 was entered into the council records:

> *We persuade our selves that you will not think us too troublesome when we assure you that nothing but the extreme necessity induces us at this time to renew our former applications. We need not say anything of what has lately happened believing you have been fully advised but we cannot avoid acquainting you that unless some speedy assistance arrives to us we can see nothing but inevitable ruin to this settlement.*
>
> *Captain Hildesley went a fortnight ago for Carolina and by means of the embargo being continued to this day the usual salt season has been lost, whereby your poor inhabitants are too likely to suffer. We are now in great want of men to defence and provisions to support us so that if we can hope for your regard it may preserve us for notwithstanding we expect a peace at hand we apprehend danger as well from the Spaniards and Pirates which nothing can free us from so well as a small ship of war.*

Finally, they did receive word that the war was over and that the Spanish were not coming to invade a second time. However, even with that worry removed Rogers still felt isolated and alone. After the *Flamborough* left in May 1720 Rogers was still sure the pirates would return and he still had heard nothing from the government. According to the Colonial State papers Rogers wrote to Secretary Craggs in November 1720 asking if the Bahamas was still part of the English government's possessions, for he had heard nothing for nineteen months.

Clearly a difficult man to deal with, Rogers fell out with Wingate Gale, captain of the *Delicia*. The ship had remained at anchor since July 1718 acting as a guardship, magazine for the garrison and sometimes a prison. Tempers were rising because of the long period of inactivity, as weeds and barnacles covered the hull growing like a disease. Finally, the tension broke when Wingate Gale refused a direct order from Rogers to come ashore. Incensed, Rogers grabbed his pistol, left his house after Gale's reply had been delivered to him, gathered up six of his best soldiers and headed for the beach. Climbing into a boat, they rowed across the harbour to the *Delicia* and went aboard. Rogers pressed home his order, Gale refused and then a scuffle occurred that had Rogers clouting Gale over the head with his pistol. Gale was arrested and taken ashore, where he was confined at the fort under guard. He was soon freed, after promising he would follow Rogers's orders and urge his crew to do the same.

By November, Rogers knew that Beauchamp had left England with several recruits for the infantry, though no one had heard from them. Intelligence from Cuba and Florida pointed to the fact that Spain might be about to resume the war, leaving the Bahamas once again exposed and ripe for taking. Every passing day Rogers was plunged deeper and deeper into debt, his bills and credit refused everywhere. Because of the new threat he was forced to keep the militia at three times the level it needed to be, which forced him to dig deep into his own pocket to maintain the garrison. Worry and exertion was wearing him down; so bad was his health that he nearly passed away twice. Finally, he had had enough of New Providence. Leaving William Fairfax as his deputy, Rogers sailed away on 6 December 1720 to Charleston, South Carolina, to recuperate.

South Carolina had also changed from being under the Lord Proprietors to a fully fledged Crown government with a commissioned Royal Governor in charge. The transition had not been easy: rioting and looting broke out. The ringleader of the disturbances was Rogers's acquaintance Captain Hildesley of the *Flamborough*. Old hatreds flared up when the two men met again and on a cold, winter morning they met each other with pistols drawn and fought a duel. The musket balls ripped into their clothes wounding each man slightly.

By February 1721 Rogers returned to Nassau, but with return to England in his mind and heart. He had done what he set out to do. The pirates were gone and no threat of war from Spain lingered around the corner. If properly supported by the British government there was no reason why the Bahamas should not flourish. Rogers's partners in London had spent over £90,000 on the colony and could spend no more. They argued for a properly incorporated company to develop the Bahamas.

In May, 1721 Rogers left Nassau and sailed for England. An article in the *London Magazine* August issue for 1721 mentioned that Woodes Rogers had returned to his home port of Bristol.

Chapter 14

Back in England

When Rogers returned to Bristol he found himself in debt and also out of a job. His partners had decided that he should not continue in his job, particularly because of his debts left in New Providence. As they saw it, they had spent more than £90,000 and had very little to show for it; but they had no idea how much had been spent in creating a defended and fortified settlement that was far better than the one Rogers originally sailed into. Nor did they really know how much he had spent of his own money. It appears that Rogers's partners tried to find long-term capital of one and a half million pounds to set up a formal trading company for the Bahamas. They were unsuccessful.

In June 1721, army officer George Phenney was appointed governor while Rogers was still on his way home. By the time Rogers arrived back in England Phenney was already on his way to his new posting with his wife.

Rogers was worn out and in debt, his health failing. He had brought a written testimonial from the council and leading citizens of the Bahamas to testify to his hard work, unstinting care and bravery shown during his two and half years in office. He sent letters in many different directions, and one, not written by Rogers but by the council and leading inhabitants of New Providence, was a testament to Rogers working so hard for the good of the settlement without regard to his fortune or his health. Another went to the Treasury. In it Rogers pleaded for an allowance to repay the money he had spent keeping the garrison fed, watered and clothed as best he could for three years. The letter recounted his recent history as well as the plea for an allowance. He also wrote another letter to his friend Vernon, who was still in the West Indies. This letter stressed that if the Bahamas were well garrisoned and supplied the colony could be extremely valuable for trade as well as strategically. He said that, if the colony were properly developed cotton, sugar and indigo could be planted and pointed out that for a secure defence to be made it would have to be from local stone. According to Rogers, with these provisions in place the Bahamas would become valuable indeed.

But the writing appeared to be in vain. The partners, also in financial straits, were unable to meet Rogers's claims and neither side could go to arbitration.

The partners could not even repay all he had spent. But the blame lies neither with Rogers nor with his partners but with a government policy that expected traders and merchants to meet the costs of expensive military defences on colonies that were tactically isolated and vulnerable. This kind of governmental thinking and behaviour would be completely inconceivable today. Yet this was the case.

The matter was left to the lawyers, since Rogers was too ill to fight it himself. In the end, in around 1723, he took the sum of £1,500 that his partners could give him, with the promise of an extra £500 if they were able to incorporate their company. No sooner had he received the money than he had to hand it over to his creditors, and found himself in a debtors' prison. But his creditors were more helpful to him than the authorities or his partners: they knew the hardships he had endured and the money he had spent; so, after taking most of his money, handed him back £400 to live on after rushing through an act of bankruptcy for the ex-governor. This got Rogers out of prison and, though very poor, enabled him to live.

As 1726 began Roger's fortunes were low indeed, but they were just beginning to look up. In July of that year he drafted a long statement of his fortunes, outlining the military actions he had taken while governor, the brief war with the Spanish from Cuba, his need to build fortifications, the pirate menace. In addition, he mentioned the financial and legal difficulties that marred his return home. This statement, now known as 'The Case of Captain Woodes Rogers, July 1726', was sent to the army authorities, who considered it for some time.

In the summer of 1727 Rogers put his case before King George II, in a letter to George Delafaye, the king's secretary. While he had been concentrating on trying to get the king's attention, the army authorities had been considering his case and they decided that the ex-governor should be made a captain of foot and placed on half pay.[35] Even better for Rogers was that his pay was backdated to 1721, the year Phenney replaced him. The army generals also recommended that Rogers be given royal favour and bounty. Rogers's captain's half pay allowed him to stay just out of poverty while he looked around for another post. That post was to return to the Bahamas.

Rogers by now was estranged from his wife. There are indications that Rogers and his wife Sarah parted company some time before 1729.[36] The reason for this supposition is that Mrs Rogers does not feature in the portrait painted of the Rogers family in 1729. By 1732 it is likely that the London addresses of Woodes and Sarah Rogers were different, which would explain why Mrs

Rogers died a widow in late 1732, the same year that Rogers himself died. His death was known in September of that year in London and it is likely that by that time they may not have known what the other was doing. If they had had no contact of any kind for all those years it is understandable that when Rogers passed away in the Bahamas in 1732 he was listed as a widower.

By the end of 1726 it looked as if there would be another war with Spain, as Spain had forged a new alliance with Austria, frightening both England and France. Flemish vessels of the Ostend East India Company sailing under the Austrian flag east into Pacific waters caused a furore with the British East India Company and in Whitehall. Stopping the flow of treasures from Peru to Spain was one way of curbing Spain's power in Europe. So before the war began a British squadron under Admiral Hosier was sent to blockade Puerto Bello for two years at a cost of 4,000 officers and men dead, not from fighting but from tropical disease.

Word got round to the British ministers that a small squadron of Spanish warships had set sail from Cadiz and was bound to sail round the Horn into the Pacific where, with its troops and artillery, it would convoy some bullion that was lying at Panama. They were to go back round the Horn to avoid Admiral Hosier and head back to Spain with their treasure.

Rogers was the foremost expert on Pacific affairs, since William Dampier was by now dead. So Lord Townshend asked Rogers what the likelihood was of the Spanish squadron getting round the Horn and bringing back the treasure at Panama. On 10 November 1726, Rogers sent back his reply. Among the many points he put forward was that the squadron had sailed for the Horn at the wrong time of year. His own experience of sailing round the Horn into the Pacific some seventeen years before now held him in good stead as he laid out his argument. He knew that with the steady Peruvian south wind and the ships laden with bullion the passage round the Horn into the Atlantic would be very hard indeed. If the silver bullion had been at Lima, he argued, it would have been easier to take it across the Andes to Buenos Aires for shipping across the Atlantic rather than trying to get round the stormy wild Horn at the tip of South America. But the war petered out in 1727 and the information that Rogers supplied was never acted on.

Meanwhile, things in the Bahamas were taking a different turn, and Rogers would head back there sooner than he thought. The Phenneys had not ingratiated themselves well with the inhabitants, and Phenney, like Rogers, had a hard time of it in Nassau. Though they had given up their piracy the men of the Bahamas were still rough sailors and spent so much of their time at sea trading or hunting for treasure round the many Spanish wrecks that it was sometimes impossible to find enough men to form a quorum for the council. Planting and tilling the soil was an anathema to them; they had never been converted to the life of agriculture, either by Rogers or Phenney.

Also like Rogers, Phenney was neglected by the British government. He only had a handful of Germans left who were able to start up plantations. Phenney went many months without a letter from home, as had Rogers. But some progress was made, and New Providence got its first church and finally a garrison chaplain, the newly ordained priest Thomas Curphey.

Phenney, a military man, saw that the fort Rogers built at Nassau had been constructed from wood and rubble and, because of the climate, was soon crumbling. Using his military experience he put his soldiers and the black slaves to work rebuilding it, creating three bastions of stone. The work was completed in 1725, but he sorely needed supplies for the fort's garrison, which was now largely made up of drunken old men who were strongly averse to hard work and discipline. Like Rogers, he faced the worry of an attack by the Spaniards. In letters home he begged for another independent company of infantry; and, again like Rogers, he heard nothing.

But Phenney's downfall was not pirates, Spaniards, drunken soldiers or lack of supplies for the settlement, but his dominating wife. He was unable to restrain her: it seems, from Colonial Office papers, that, among other illegal activities, she had her hand in private schemes for trading with the Spanish on Cuba. In 1728 a raft of complaints against her from the female population of the Bahamas reached London. Her chief accuser was one Mrs Martha Vere, an islander who travelled to London in person to have her grievances heard. She poured out the jealousies and intrigues experienced by the women of New Providence. Mrs Phenney, she claimed, had taken control, privately, of the shopkeeping trade on the island: she claimed the governor's wife had a monopoly on the sale of all provisions on New Providence, especially biscuit and rum, which she sold by the pint.

The accusation was also personal. Mrs Vere claimed that Mrs Phenney had wrecked her own domestic situation by luring away one of her indentured servants before his time was over. Among her other allegations was that the Phenneys had forced her to stay in the Bahamas when many other settlers were leaving to go to Bermuda because of the treatment they were receiving from Mrs Phenney. She also accused Mrs Phenney of perverting the course of justice by browbeating juries and threatening magistrates.

The lords of the Board of Trade and Plantations could not overlook the allegations. Unfortunately for the Phenneys, the Chaplain Thomas Curphey was also in London. His statement was taken, corroborating everything that Mrs Vere had written and said about Mrs Phenney. He asked for time to put his thoughts down on paper: in the meantime more people were heard.

While all this was going on Rogers was still trying to find another position that would get him back to respectability. In Feburary 1728 he had received a testimonial detailing his financial losses, praising his service to the Crown, the sacrifices he had made, his devotion to his office and his constant loyalty to the Crown. This testimonial was signed by the great and the good of English commerce and politics of the day. The Duke of Montague, who had large West Indian holdings, praised his resolution and fidelity, as did Michaj Perry, an eminent London West Indian merchant, important Bristol merchants, Edward Southwell, George Earle and Hugh Raymond, an old friend of Rogers and a London merchant. Other figures who added their names to the testimonial included former governors of Virginia, Massachusetts and Bermuda, together with Vernon.

The testimonial went a long way to helping Rogers to get back on his feet fully again, and it was given to the lords of the Board of Trade and Plantations for their consideration. In the meantime, they heard from supporters of Mrs Phenney, who claimed that Mrs Vere was weak and not of right mind, so much so that no black slave could possibly obey her. Others praised Mr Phenney as being the best governor ever sent across the Atlantic, while others attempted to paint Mrs Phenney as a selfless, caring and law-abiding woman.

But despite these arguments Chaplain Thomas Curphey in his own statement used his religious authority to support Mrs Vere's allegations. He confirmed what she said and went further by saying that New Providence required a more orderly civil government and that a house of assembly be set up in New Providence ending with the fact that several settlers had decided not to settle in New Providence because of the illegal and arbitrary behaviour of Mrs Phenney. None of the mud flung at her stuck at all to her husband; he was universally seen as a man of good character.

On 1 October 1728 the lords submitted what Curphey had said, along with other statements to the government, with a request that the government of the Bahamas be put into steadier hands.

King George II, through the offices of the then Secretary of State, the Duke of Newcastle, was coming to the same conclusion but from a different direction, that of Admiral Sir Charles Wager. He was an old friend of Woodes Rogers who had been on the West Indies station twenty years before and one of Rogers's partners in his 1718 expedition to New Providence. By 1728 he was living in London and was soon to be made First Lord of the Admiralty. He gave Rogers a strong letter of support and urged him to hand it to the Duke of Newcastle. Dated 10 August 1728, the letter's main argument was that the Board of Trade had not yet heard about Rogers's claim to go back to New Providence. They were still embroiled at the time with the claims of Mrs Vere and the Phenneys' friends.

Two days after he received Wager's letter supporting him, Rogers sent it to the Duke of Newcastle's secretary at Hampton Court. The duke was in attendance on the king and Rogers hoped that this would speed up his claim for his old job as governor of the Bahamas. Rogers wrote that he hoped that, as Walpole's government had promised him re-employment and he had so many backers like Admiral Wager, he would not have to wait long for news.

The wheels of patronage and pressure had been properly oiled, and so he did not have to wait long. On 18 October Woodes Rogers was again appointed as governor of the Bahamas. This time was different: the position of governor now carried an annual salary of £400 and there was no Bahamas Company to get in the way of governing.

Rogers would return to Nassau, but not with the problems he had experienced first time round, which had nearly killed him and brought him home to debtors' prison. He would be facing entirely different challenges.

Chapter 15

The Governor Returns

In the summer of 1729 Rogers was busy in London preparing to return to the Bahamas as governor. His salary would last his full term in office. His main concern was still boosting the economy of the settlement, trying to build trade and, of course, ensuring he had adequate defences against the Spanish. After his original handling of the pirates he could be sure that the threat of pirates returning was no longer paramount; but should the defences seem lacking or weak then anything could happen.

Rogers took his eldest son with him to the Bahamas. This time there were no white settlers, no cattle or costly stores to go with him, but there were gifts from the king for the garrison chapel. A generous £200 was laid out for these gifts, a Bible and two large prayer-books, sumptuous crimson cushions and cloth for the pulpit, a pair of cushions for the reading desk, a carpet for the altar and a crimson damask with fringes of silk. The altar was also to have two linen cloths. In addition there were a chalice, a paten, two small flagons and an alms dish.

Before he sailed, Rogers sat for his portrait, the only one ever done of him, painted by Hogarth. He was 50 years old, and the look that the painter gave him was one of serene confidence. He may have had some scars from the musket ball that struck his jaw, but these do not appear in the painting.

Confident and happy as he embarked for the Bahamas, he had no idea of the trouble he was sailing into. In May he had met the Board of Trade and Plantations to discuss the names of the council in the Bahamas. From Rogers's knowledge of the local personalities there he suggested the councillors should have seniority according to their abilities and also asked that John White, a London trader, should be included in the selection in place of another nominee who had died.[37]

After all his debts had been paid along with his expenses he made a new will, leaving what was left of his estate to William Whetstone Rogers, his eldest son, who was now sailing with him to the Bahamas, and also to Sarah Rogers, who could have been either his wife or daughter.

On 26 May he set sail. In his party were three men, John White, his son and an associate of White's, a London businessman named John Colebrooke, who would become Rogers's nemesis. There were no soldiers sailing with them this time, even though Rogers had put in a request for another independent company.

After a stormy voyage, Rogers and his party arrived in Nassau on 25 August 1729, according to Colonial Office papers. They found the island battered and bruised from a hurricane that had hammered the settlement in July, and summer fever was rife. Some things had changed and others remained the same. The problems of defence and regular settlement that he had experienced during his first governorship were still prevalent. Governor Phenney had improved the walls of the fort but its living quarters were still very poor. Phenney had also designed and built an elaborate gateway, but the harbour had changed little. A small church had been built behind the waterside, along with Government House. Within the garrison itself was the new chapel, which was very plain; so the gifts Rogers brought from the king would enhance it dramatically. Government House was to be Rogers's residence in the Bahamas. It was a two-storey comfortable dwelling in the Georgian style.

His first task was to get rid of the Phenneys, and before he could do that there were expenses to be met. In order to build the bastions of the fort Phenney had raised his money locally from the Bahamian residents, who had turned from piracy only when Rogers was first governor – they were not used to paying taxes, and much resentment against Phenney had been built up. They claimed that the money had been raised illegally because, even though the money had been used for the public good, there was no assembly. The total amount claimed was £1,200; there was no way that Rogers could cover that claim. 'It was desired that Mr Phenney might be called to account for the money raised for the public service and obliged to reimburse what was illegally raised and received by him,' the clerk of the council entered into the record book. 'Captain Rogers declined it but has taken security till the King's Pleasure be known.'

The new governor did all he could to treat the unpopular Phenneys with respect, but the shouts and cries of the Bahamians for recompense was too much, and Rogers gave in. Phenney had to draw up a bond for the full amount and was obliged to raise sureties against it; so when he returned to England he found himself handing over his estate to the guarantors. By 1731, according to the papers from the Board of Trade and Plantations, he was declared to have acted properly when raising taxes, and the bond Rogers had set he was duly bound to cancel.

To make matters worse, Rogers also became embroiled in the Phenneys' marriage, one filled with rancour, tension and dispute. The couple had fallen out, and Phenney himself went to Rogers, begging him to keep Mrs Phenney on the island while he fled to England, where he would then gather all the evidence he needed to push for a divorce.

Clearly wanting to be rid of them both, Rogers agreed to Phenney's proposal but before anything could be done, Mrs Phenney, hearing of her husband's plot with the new governor, counter-attacked. Eventually, the Phenneys boarded a ship in November, and sailed together for South Carolina and on to London. Rogers wrote about the Phenneys to Admiral Wager's secretary, expecting them to conspire against him; this they did, after they arrived home.

Once again, Rogers turned his attention to the defences of the garrison and to the trade and welfare of his settlement. The cannon he had in the fort were close to useless when he arrived, chiefly because the timber of the gun carriages had rotted away since Rogers's first term as governor. Most of the cannon lay strewn along the ramparts, the carriages collapsed under them.

Accounts of a wide variety of topics were entered into the council records. Here is an abstract of the account of the fortifications Rogers submitted to the Board of Trade and Plantations. It shows Rogers's frustration at the lack of improvement or action taken by Phenney: 'His [Rogers's] frustration and disappointment at his predecessor having sold the Iron Work for the large Carriages for £100 which he hopes will be thought just to be allowed him. No Carriages being left fit for Service and the place left in worse state of defence than 8 years ago. He hopes to have 50 guns mounted by the spring and represents what works he thinks necessary and would complete had he means to do it. He promises a further account and estimate of the charges and what the country can and may be willing to contribute.'

The same entry goes on to talk about the independent company from Bermuda which were very short of their complement, 'mostly of old men and though a great charge to recruit he hopes soon to fill it up and make it more serviceable. His own company is as complete as any in America though 23 men were lost last year.'

The timber used for the guard room and officers' quarters that Rogers had built had been blown down and destroyed by the hurricane, and he knew he had to rebuild them before he could send for his new independent company of infantry from Bermuda.

An entry in the records of the assembly illustrates his urgent need to rebuild the fortifications. 'He [Rogers] defers sending for the Independent Company from Bermuda till the Fort, Guard Rooms and more damaged by a late hurricane can be repaired and he hopes to do it in a months time having hired a vessel for that purpose. He expects new inhabitants from Bermuda and the Leeward Islands. He don't doubt raising sufficient quantities of Provisions and other commodities necessary for Trade when they come. Provisions are now scarce and Trade is at a low ebb.'

When eventually the independent company did arrive, they turned out to be a sorry lot indeed, weak, elderly and unfit for military use. He had had no idea what they would be like, but he knew that he had to start rebuilding, so he used local rather than imported wood. But once again he ran into the same labour problem that he had experienced as governor before. He could only count on the black slaves and what was left of his soldiers to do the heavy and hard work.

Determined to widen the Bahamas trade outlets, which proved to be difficult indeed, Rogers also needed to call an assembly as soon as he could to fulfil his promise. Once the main damage from the hurricane was repaired, he finally did so, on 29 September 1729 – and things started to go badly from that moment on. The council had been sitting before the assembly was called, and Rogers's son, William Whetstone Rogers, was its clerk. The following excerpt is from a letter Rogers wrote to the Board of Trade and Plantations dated 12 November 1729 telling them of the first Assembly: 'The inhabitants were very much pleased with the appointment of an assembly who met for the first time on the 30th of September and the following proposed 12 Acts whereof are enclosed and will send the Acts so soon as they can be transcribed.' The assembly itself comprised twenty-four people and had the power to make laws and ordnances along the same lines as those in Great Britain.[38] No Parliament building existed for this first session, so it took place in the house of Samuel Lawford.

Another entry, dated 11 October 1730, is an account of the state of the settlement after its battering by the hurricane and the challenges Rogers faced. The Acts of Assembly had been delayed, as the record indicates:

> He [Rogers] has received the Board's letter of the 24 April last and is very sorry the Acts of Assembly were not forwarded till now and gives account of his being disappointed therein in sending other papers and he hopes the delay will have no ill consequences.
>
> He depends upon more frequent conveyances for the future and promises duplicates of the Acts now sent and what he may have to do in about a month.

He found the places so poor and thin of inhabitants that he never mentioned any salary to them for himself or any other. The fees of all Officers there are the lowest in the Americas and no officer can support himself thereon without some other employment. The accounts of money saved since his arrival and he hopes to prevail on the Assembly that most of it may be applied towards the fortifications that are in great want of it.

He refers to some enclosed remarks on the condition of the fort and about the great expense he has been at for the barracks.

Little progress yet made in New Improvements but since the Act to encourage the raising of Cotton more has been planted than for some years past and more and larger vessels are now being built than have been there ten years. They having the best timber than in any part of America.

Since he arrived two plantations have begun to raise sugar canes. Of late one of the inhabitants best employement was sawing Mahogony and Madera Planks.

However, that land soon proved to be useless for sugar, as a later account from the record book shows. 'Their lands at New Providence prove not so fit for sugar cane as has been reported and is good but in few places, the inland being generally worse than near the waters side. Some persons from St Christopher could not find sufficient land lying any where for intended sugar work. Cat Island is reported to be the best land of the Bahamas and several people who have no land at St Christophers would remove thence to settle it.'

There was also the question of the chaplain. 'The inhabitants are in great want of a Chaplain who might be handsomely supported and the whole colony has desired him [Rogers] to apply for one.'

If these troubles were not enough, things were about to get worse for Rogers. The Speaker of the House and the man who would soon dominate the Assembly and cause so much grief for Rogers was the newly arrived John Colebrooke, who had befriended Rogers's son. This man was a rogue, intent on power without any regard to how his actions affected others.

To get the measure of the man we need to go back a few years. In 1721 when John Ker from Kersland in Scotland, an adventurer and sailor himself with an abiding hatred of the English, was busy trying to set up the Ostend East India Company under the flag of Imperial Austria, to counter English trade in the West Indies and American colonies, he was in Brussels making as many connections as he could with people like Count Windischgratz and Field

Marshal Vellon, illustrious members of the Austrian court.

Ker's idea was to establish a free port for the Americas at New Providence under Austrian rule. At this time Brussels was the capital of the Austrian Netherlands and it was here that Ker met Colebrooke. Both men lodged in the same house in Brussels and Colebrooke did all he could to find out what Ker's business was. Finally, Colebrooke found out through Ker's secretary, and so Ker had to take the man into his confidence in order to keep his scheme as quiet as he could. Colebrooke achieved this by using and pretending to love Ker's secretary. Ker may have thought that Colebrooke might be useful in running the eastern part of the trade, and we can assume that he talked about the idea of the free port at New Providence to Colebrooke. Of course when the two men parted, Ker managed to get a promise of silence from Colebrooke.

But the promise was soon broken. Indeed, Colebrooke double-crossed Ker by going to Windischgratz and Vellon himself, convincing them that he was the main protagonist and that Ker was just a sideshow. So well did he convince these two men that they sent him to Vienna to talk to the Foreign Minister, Count Zinzendorff, about his plans. While in Vienna, Colebrooke made close contact with Francis Coleman, a senior member of the British Embassy, and boasted about how well connected he was at the Austrian Imperial Court, about the Ostend East India Company scheme and announced to Coleman that the company's charter had been granted. The Ostend East India Company never really came to anything.

But Colebrooke was not all he appeared to be. His credit slumped and when he arrived back in Brussels in 1723 he was one step ahead of the authorities who had been ordered to seize him and his papers. This manipulative, scheming and slippery man managed to get away and began to travel, only to end up six years later as Woodes Rogers's right-hand man and trading partner to his son, Whetstone, in his new venture in the Bahamas.

Colebrooke brought long commercial experience to the table and had circulated in some of the most sophisticated European circles. But since the call for his arrest one could assume he made the Bahamas trip because he was on the run and could not return to Europe. Colonial State papers describe Colebrooke as being of pleasant conversation and good sense.

Such a man would have no problem in dominating and influencing such rough and simple seafarers as he found at New Providence. He schemed to dominate the Bahamas and turn them into the free port for the Americas along the lines that Ker had envisaged. His chief target was Woodes Rogers.

Colebrooke's plan was to dominate the Assembly: to do that he had John

White as his chief ally. He made White the second senior member of the council and its Treasurer and Chief Justice. Another ally, Jenner, was made secretary to the governor to complete Colebrooke's spider's web.

A loyal and staunch support of Rogers, Lewis Bonnet, wrote to Delafaye (the Duke of Newcastle's secretary) that the two merchants made Rogers uneasy, especially so as many of the men in the Assembly were soon corrupted by Colebrooke and White to turn against Rogers. 'At the late sessions of Assembly the Governor recommended the state of the fortifications being much out of repair (the state of which is enclosed) which the Assembly were willing to comply with but were diverted from it by the insinuation of Mr Colebrook, their speaker, much to the prejudice of the colony upon which he dissolved them.' At this first point when Colebrooke began to flex his muscles we see Rogers dissolving the Assembly outright, then calling for elections. The account entered in the records shows Colebrooke at work:

> *Another Assembly is elected whom he finds of the same stamp with the last by the instigation of the said Colebrooke, who has convinced the most ignorant of them with the notions of their being subject to the Garrison – it being a power that aught to be opposed. He never received any complaints against the Garrison since his arrival.*
>
> *Mr Colebrook attempts to take from the Officers and Soldiers that are freeholder, the liberty of voting. He, Rogers, expects but little good from the present Assembly who oppose any allowance be given towards the fortifications. Mr White and Mr Jenner, Members of the council assist Mr Colebrooke in his measures. He desires the said members to retire into another room whilst he advised with the rest of the council on the subject of fortifications.*
>
> *At the same time they received a message from the assembly relating thereto and having converted with the members present he, Rogers, sent for Mr White to make up a Board but found he was gone to Mr Colebrooke's and being summoned the next morning he refused to attend. Whereupon having taken the advice of the council present the Governor suspended him till His Majesty's pleasure shall be known.*

Tension in the Assembly grew, and Rogers soon began to realize that he was up against a far more shrewd and formidable opponent than Hornigold and Vane ever were.

The first few months of the Assembly were calm while Colebrooke made his plans and gathered together his allies. Several acts were passed to push forward the economy of the island. The planting of cotton was an act of the Assembly and Colebrooke and young Rogers began their partnership for creating plantations and for a house of trade. Rogers's son built a two-masted trading vessel, the *Providence*, with six guns to protect other traders. Indeed, more vessels were built and launched in Nassau than had been for many years. Colebrooke and Whetstone Rogers sent to West Africa for more black slaves, as only they could work on the plantations.

But before the year was over, young Rogers and Colebrooke's partnership was in ruin. In a letter dated 14 October 1730 (now in London's Maritime Museum) Woodes Rogers wrote to his old friend Admiral Wager saying he could not proceed as well as he thought he could because of Colebrooke's machinations.

By the end of 1730 the Assembly was torn apart with strife and conflict, most of it made by the unreasonable Colebrooke. Rogers could see that the soldiers' quarters at the garrison were so bad that he needed to raise money to rebuild them, and he knew he needed to raise the money locally. Colebrooke hated the garrison and refused to spend any money on rebuilding it. He considered it a curb on the liberty and freedom of all Bahamians and so opposed any plans that Rogers had to rebuild the fortifications, delaying the passing of any motions that pertained to this policy in the Assembly.

'The Governor has published His Majesty's Order of the 25th of September transmitted from the Duke of Newcastle since which they have lost two Sloops, one of which is carried to the Havanas,' the chief clerk recorded. 'The Governor appointed Mr White the forementioned Chief Justice, and for his partiality displaced him, who he believes is come to England to Misconstrue his actions, having lately misconstrued everything he has done for the public services. He begs leave of the Board for him to answer any complaints that shall be made against him whose patronage and protection he desires.'

As tensions rose Rogers lost his temper, and with his authority as Royal Governor dissolved the Assembly. Outraged, Colebrooke took all the books and papers that recorded the Assembly's actions to his home and flatly refused to give them to Rogers when he sent for them. Colebrooke then began accusing Rogers of arbitrary and tyrannical rule. The worst was still to come.

By now Thomas Curphey had left as chaplain of the garrison and so services in the chapel, newly adorned by its gifts from the king, were read by an army officer. This did not go down very well with anyone. Colonial Office papers show that Rogers made an urgent request for another chaplain.

The interior of New Providence was rocky and there were only a few places where the soil was good enough for planting. Cat Island was the most promising and most fertile island in the Bahamas, certainly for the planting of sugar. But Rogers had to see it for himself so he decided to get preparations under way for visiting the island, but he needed instructions to begin working it; and once the work started, it would need to be inhabited and protected. But before he could do this his health began to fail again in the early months of 1731. He decided he needed to go to South Carolina to recuperate and obtain the legal and spiritual reinforcements he knew he would need. 'The Governor heard that two sixty-gun ships have arrived at the Havana and that they have increased the number of forces in that city and that the *Adventure* man of war lay ready to sail with the money saved out of the Spanish Wreck for Cadiz,' the chief clerk recorded. 'The Governor intends for the perfection of his health to go to South Carolina and return back in three weeks and hopes that one or two of His Majesty's ships will attend him in order to make a demand of some vessels taken by the Spaniards.' By March Rogers was in Charleston.

Rogers achieved three things with his visit to South Carolina. He recovered his health and he managed to get another chaplain for the garrison chapel and, more importantly, a good lawyer to deal with Colebrooke. Rogers wrote to the Board of Trade and Plantations that he hoped he would soon be sending more promising accounts of how things fared on New Providence. At the time of this letter he had not yet visited Cat Island, but proposed that he would go there.

By early May, fit and feeling much more confident with his new lawyer, Rogers was back in Nassau. He found that Colebrooke, far from being idle during his absence, had been whipping up dissent with the inhabitants of the island, breeding disturbances and encouraging unrest amongst the soldiers of the garrison. Rogers appointed his new South Carolina lawyer as Attorney General, and in his new capacity he immediately transferred the fight between the two men into the courts. A Grand Jury was convened, spurned by Colebrooke's supporters as being rigged. Sessions were held at the end of May. Colebrooke was found guilty of vexatious litigation, fined £750 and put in jail.

This was not the end of the matter. Colebrooke appealed against his sentence and his friends began to intimidate the jurors, persuading them to go back on their views. But Rogers released Colebrooke on bail, binding him to stay on New Providence. Rogers sent a letter to the Duke of Newcastle on 10

June reporting the trial while Colebrooke locked himself in his house for weeks to work on his own defence. Refusing to appeal in the official way he spent more than three weeks writing the justification of his actions.

Slyly, Colebrooke hired a small ship in another man's name giving her papers for a voyage no further than Bermuda when in fact she was headed for the Atlantic and for England. This was to ensure the fruits of his labours were sent to the Board of Trade and Plantations. Fortunately, Rogers discovered Colebrooke's plan and sent a letter of his own to Delafaye on the same ship on 29 June. In this letter, Rogers stated he had 'never had so much uneasiness in my life as he has occasioned here'.

In mid-July the ship sailed. A month later Rogers decided to send his son home where he could formally end his partnership with Colebrooke, take with him all the papers pertaining to the trial of Colebrooke and also ensure the prompt and accurate answering of any allegations that Colebrooke may have levelled against him. Rogers was sure that no governor could function unless Colebrooke was somehow constrained: this comes through in an entry in the council records:

> *The Governor mentions his letter of August last sent with Mr Colebrook's appeal to His Majesty and desires the Board that if the said Colebrook or any one else should complain of him that his Son may answer for him. He has transmitted the council's proceedings and answers to queries and an account of the families and having advised with the council the properest method to get people to settle there, they are of the opinion the only way is for His Majesty to take it under his protection, continual disputes arising between the proprietors, agents and the people about the property of lands which discourages them.*
>
> *The influence Mr Colebrook had over the last Assembly was the reason of their not complying with His Majesty's instructions and till he hears from the Board he does not intend to call one lest the said Colebrooke should have the same power. The inhabitants not being willing to assist in repairing the fortifications it will easily be taken on in case of war.*

While the Assembly remained dissolved Rogers could concentrate on trying to build the settlement's economy and work on improving the social affairs of the islands. He wrote to the Board of Trade and Plantations on 14 October 1731 giving his latest accounts of his governorship. The settlement was still very small. On New Providence only 800 acres had been cultivated, while little more had been planted on Harbour Island and Eleuthera Island. He never got a chance to visit Cat Island, which at this time remained unpopulated and uncultivated. The population numbered 633 whites and 409 black slaves on New Providence. William Whetstone Rogers with his nominal partner Colebrooke were the largest landowners and had thirty black slaves while the second largest landowner, Colonel Richard Thompson, had twenty-two. Harbour Island had a total population of 169, Eleuthera only 162.

The remaining Germans had either died or left the islands. They had been the best settlers and had kept the village of Nassau supplied with corn. Colebrooke, currying favour with the rougher elements of the waterside, purposely undercut the Germans with imported corn until all the settlers had left in despair. Once they had gone, Colebrooke enjoyed a monopoly and sold his corn for double the price of the locally grown corn the Germans had supplied. The immigrants from other parts of the West Indies who had come to the Bahamas to plant sugar discovered that the soil was no good for that crop and so they too sailed away.

By 1732 the threat of the pirates had gone, as had the threat of the Spanish attacking from Cuba. Rogers should have expected that the coming years would show a steady increase in the prosperity of the islands. But nothing had been heard from Rogers since his letter of October.

Then, on 20 July, Richard Thompson sent a letter to the Secretary of State simply stating that the governor of the Bahamas, Woodes Rogers, had died on 5 July. There was no reason given for his death in the letter, nothing to say he died of illness or natural causes, though we can speculate that the tropical illness that had been his enemy for so many years had finally claimed him. We know from Colonial Office papers that a funeral was held for him in Nassau; the September issue of the *Gentleman's Magazine* recorded his death.

Successive governors also came to loggerheads with Colebrooke. Rogers's own successor was Richard Fitzwilliam, who had been the Surveyor General of Customs in the Carolinas and had also taken an interest in the Bahamas. The new governor almost immediately ran into trouble with Colebrooke, who kept the islands in a state of turmoil and, as the books of Assembly that recorded all its Acts had been stolen, none could be enacted. But one night, one lone piece of paper, one document was dropped off at the door of Government House. A few years later, however, Colebrooke's name disappeared from the membership of the Assembly. In 1734 his brother James wrote to the Duke of Newcastle's secretary Delafaye that his brother, John, had been forced to quit his plantations in the Bahamas. It seems that Colebrooke may finally have met his match with the governors who succeeded Rogers.

What legacy does Woodes Rogers leave behind? Was he a hero? The answer to that has to be yes. He was a trail-blazer, a leader of men, a visionary and has every right to stand tall with the best of British heroes. As governor of New Providence he cleared away the pirates, the thorn in the side of the entire merchant community in Britain who traded throughout the West Indies. His determination to rid the islands of the pirates, forcing them to go elsewhere and turning them from their rough ways to become law-abiding citizens made sure that Britain's American and West Indies trade, which was far more important than it is today, continued to flourish.

He touched history and influenced the future of the West Indies and of Great Britain. But he is virtually unknown, overshadowed by Blackbeard, Captain Kidd and people like Charles Vane. Such men were no heroes – Rogers truly was.

Appendix 1

The Trial of William Whaling

The following account of the trial of William Whaling, a citizen of the settlement on New Providence, has been included to provide the reader with an idea of the kind of rough justice that had to be meted out as well as some of the mundane issues that Rogers and his council faced. This was one of the first things he had to take care of during his first time as governor of the Bahamas.

The trial took place on 4 March 1718 at the guard room before

> *His Excellency Woodes Rogers Esq. Governor, Robert Beauchamp, William Fairfax, Wingate Gale, Mathew Taylor and Thomas Proctor.*
>
> *The court being sat and the grand jury sworn in a small time after they had, with reason returned to the court and presented two bills of indictment against William Whaling for feloniously stealing and carrying away a hickory stick with a silver head to the value of two shillings sixpence, two gold spangles to the value of one shilling and three pence, one piece of Kurdish holland to the value of ten shillings, one remnant of silk satinette to the value of ten shillings, three pair of Gloves to the value of three shilling and six pence, one strip of holland watercoat to the value of five shillings, three silver spoons to the value of one pound ten shillings, one silver plate to the value of one pound ten shillings, the goods and ware belonging to Mathew Mayfair Gent and also one leatherette coat to the value of ten shillings belonging to Lieutenant Henson, Marine, which all goods were taken out of the house of John Pearson on about the sixth day of December.*
>
> *The second indictment against William Whaling was for maliciously and feloniously setting fire to and burning the house belonging to John Pearson aforesaid.*
>
> *The prisoner pleaded not guilty.*

Everything was done the way it would have been done in England, using English laws, rules, procedures and traditions. The minutes of the trial indicate that the members of the jury were Robert Lorey, Doinijah Stanbury, Humphrey Moxy, Eric Hancock, William Bridger, David Harinwood, Joseph Bottle, Philip Hall, Moses Sims, Joseph Sims, and William Devain:

Which sat in rows being sworn and challenged as made by the Prisoner, the Court proceeded and called for the Prosecutor. Then the Prosecutor, John Pearson, was sworn and examined and deposed that on or about the time of six and nine in the evening the said John Pearson and his wife Sarah were at the house[39] of their neighbours when and where the Prosecutor was told but by whom he could not recollect that his house was then on fire and found the prisoner lying on a chart near the place where the house was burnt and that the Prosecutor verily believed had set the house on fire though he feigned himself to be too drunk. Then the Prosecutor saved very little of his household furniture and particularly sought for but could not find a certain chest where he put his money. But the day after walking with his wife through the bushes behind the place where on his house did stand found the chest broken open and the bag empty of the money being about twenty five pounds and some rings but no appearance as if any fire had touched the chest and to smother his act set fire to the house that he might better conceal the theft of the money.

Conran Winter being sworn for the King and examined said that the prisoner at the bar brought a silver head of a stick to him and desired him to accept there of as a present which Conran received and gave the prisoner a bag of pounds but afterwards hearing that John Pearsons house was burnt and several things of value suspected to be stolen hence showed the silver head to the Prosecutor who immediately said to Conran that the silver head belonged to mrs Mathew Maysson who had left it in his care whereupon Conran deliverd the silver head to the Prosecutor with the intelligence of the prisoner of whom he had it and further said as he knowed not.

Thomas Ferril being sworn for the King and examined said that to the best of his knowledge the silver head of the stick which the prisoner at the bar gave to Edward Conran is the same one that Thomas Ferril gave to Mathew Maysson and also that the said Ferril bought two gold spangles of Samuel Lawarence, a companion of his in company with the prisoner at the bar for a weeks worth of sugar. And further that the said Thomas Ferril, suspecting the said spangles to be stolen made due enquiries of John MacKenzie, the goldsmith, if he owned them who directed him, the said

Ferril, to the Prosecutor John Pearson who upon view of the said spangles affirmed him to be the owner thereof for which the said, Ferril delivered the said spangles to the said Prosecutor and further says not.

Ann Whitehead being sworn for the King and examined said that on or about the twenty fifth day of December last the prisoner at the bar came to her house with a remnant of about four square of Kenting cloth which the same bought for ten shillings and that about a day or so afterwards the said prisoner brought to the said, Ann Whitehead, a remnant of stuff which she also bought for ten shillings and afterwards the prisoner at the bar on another day presented her with three pairs of women's leather gloves, which goods and wares so come by she made the discovery of to the Prosecutor after she heard his house being burnt and robbed and also that one Henry Hawkins told her, the said Ann Whitehead, that the prisoner at the bar gave him a waste coat and further said she not.

Sarah Pearson being sworn for the King and examined declared that the coat mentioned by Ann Whitehead belonged to John Hewson a friend of the said Mathew Maysson, and those things, with other apparel, were left in a chest under the care of the said, Sarah Pearson, and further said that the pair of breeches and some handkerchiefs which she had lost were found onboard the vessel that the prisoner at the bar was bound in from Providence and were presented to her. Sarah Pearson further deposed that the prisoner at the bar was with her in the house, being a logder in the afternoon and saw her put money into that chest, which was afterwards found in the bushes and when she went out of the house she left the prisoner therein, and that no fire or candle had been in the house sometime before, or at her going out, and that the spangles aforementioned were in the same chest where the money was lodged and taken away.

Then the prisoner at the bar was asked if he had anything to say or any witnesses to call in his defence and answering that he had not coming the taking and dispersing of the several things aforementioned but denied that he burnt the house.

The newly arrived governor, Rogers, looked over the jury and summed up the evidence against Whaling. He told the jury they must give the court a just verdict. At that point, the jury retired, returning about two hours later. William Whaling was brought in. The jury reached a verdict of guilty on Whaling on all the charges against him. Whaling was then asked by Rogers if he had anything to say and why the sentence of death should not be passed upon him. Whaling replied he had nothing to say: 'But the court observing that the prisoner, during the time of trial, appeared to be very sullen and obstinate was willing to show the prisoner such clemency as might soften his suffering and sense of his guilt so gave him respite till next morning and leave to send for any friend to advise him.'

The following morning, Whaling was again brought into the court and asked by Rogers if he had anything to say; again, Whaling replied he had nothing to say. Rogers then turned to the court and pronounced the sentence of death on Whaling, who was taken back to the place where he had been imprisoned, under guard at the fort. He was hung at eleven o'clock on the morning of 21 March 1718.

Appendix 2

A Letter to the King

The following is a letter written by the council on New Providence to the King of England, outlining some of the difficulties they faced in keeping the settlement going in the face of great odds. As we have seen, Rogers always took great pains to ensure that everyone knew how much sustaining the colony was costing him.

Most Gracious Sovereign

We Your Majesty's most dutiful loyal subjects do out of the deepest sense of gratitude, acknowledge Your Majesty's goodness to us in re-establishing this government of these islands which have been ruined through the long want thereof.

This island of New Providence being situated near the centre of Your Majesty's American dominion maybe very advantageously improved by enjoying the benefit of Your Majesty's garrison thereon, soon was made capable to curb the neighbouring Spaniards and annoy or prevent any enemy that may attempt to disturb Your Majesty's plantations or subjects trading to the most valuable parts of America.

We humbly hope for Your Majesty's fatherly help to enable us to perform our several duties and then we hope there will be no reason to fear the pirates sheltering anymore amongst these islands and parts adjacent and we doubt not the remonstrances from Jamaica and most of Your Majesty's governments will for the future oblige the commanders of the ships of war to a stricter execution of their orders which would very much contribute to the security of Your Majesty's colonies and prevention of piracy.

The unavailable charge that the works of the fortification have obliged us to be at has been as frugally applied as the miserable circumstances of the place could allow. And the interest of several worthy gentlemen, adventured hither, was considerably more use of to secure this settlement in the most dangerous times when we could have no other relief relying on Your Majesty's great goodness, that when that charge is before Your Sacred Majesty for your Royal consideration it will be recommended to the parliament that those honourable gentlemen may be reimbursed their money so expended for the public good.

May Your Majesty enjoy a long and happy life and the crown of Great Britain deserve that we and all your subjects may ever be the happiest people under the greatest of monarchs.

Appendix 3

Navigational Aids

The Davis Quadrant was invented by a celebrated navigator of the time of Queen Elizabeth I and was the best navigation tool around. It was also known as the Back Staff because the observer had his back to the sun in order to use it. Another navigational aid at the time was the Cross Staff, in use since the days of Columbus and a very simple affair. It was a four-sided, hardwood straight staff three feet long, with four sliding cross-pieces called ten, thirty, sixty and ninety, which were placed along the staff according to the altitude of the sun or the star, depending on the time. A scale of minutes and degrees intersected with the cross-pieces and gave the angle that provided the observer with an indication of the ship's position.

The Almacantas staff was another navigational aid used just after sunrise and just before sunset to find the sun's azimuth and the variations of the compass. With such primitive navigation aids, finding landfall as accurately as Rogers and his men did was no mean achievement.

Notes

1 Including *A New Voyage around the World* (1697) and *A Voyage to New Holland* (1699).

2 Throughout this book, spellings of material quoted from Woodes Rogers's letters and journal have been modernized, for ease of understanding.

3 On his own voyage round the world Rogers did not work in this way. He relied on captured ships to act as their supply and hospital ships.

4 Taken from *Life Aboard a British Privateer in the Time of Queen Anne*, by Robert Leslie, published in 1864.

5 This is how Rogers spells it in his journal.

6 Careening is a nautical term for cleaning the bottom of ships. The ship has to be taken out of the water or at the very least put over on to a 45 degree angle so the undersides of the hull can be scraped and cleaned.

7 Presumably this was so they wouldn't have to continue the voyage, or in case they died!

8 Rogers often refers to lifeboats as pinnaces. The *Duke* carried a pinnace, a small sailing vessel that would have been hoisted off and onboard the ship or towed behind the frigate. He used it for a wide variety of purposes. However, the ship also carried rowing boats or lifeboats. It is sometimes difficult to know which boat he is referring to in his journal.

9 A slender double-reeded instrument, or oboe.

10 Rogers spells this as 'Alcatros', which is derived from the Spanish word Alcatraz, the name for a large water fowl, a word the Spanish and the Portuguese extended to cover any waterfowl.

11 Reefing a sail is to reduce the working area of a sail by lowering it part way.

12 On his return to England, Rogers discovered this ship was the *Cinque Ports*, a ship on which Alexander Selkirk had been one of the senior officers before being marooned on Juan Fernández. Captain Stradling who had abandoned Selkirk had been imprisoned by the Spanish for four years.

13 A two-masted sailing boat which, according to Rogers's journal, seems to be in addition to the pinnace carried by the *Duke*, as he makes reference to both vessels being sent out one after the other.

14 This was before the arrival of Rogers with Dampier on board. Captain Dampier had been to the island in 1684 and also with the *Cinque Ports* but was not aboard that ship when Selkirk was abandoned.

15 At Lobos they built a large launch for landing men, which was later used in the sack of Guayaquil.

16 These birds were probably a flock of Gallenazo, which Darwin described as

frequenting the woods on the west coast of South America (see Leslie, *Life Aboard a British Privateer*).

17 This was the Bishop of Chokeaqua, who was on his way from Spain to take up his residency at the bishopric, which, according to Rogers, was a place far up the country in the southern part of Peru. The bishop was said to be carrying upwards of 200,000 pieces of eight and a large quantity of gold. He was to have travelled in the *Ascensión* but because it leaked so he switched to another ship, the *Havre de Grace*, French-built under a Spanish flag.

18 Although it is difficult to fathom from Rogers's journal, it appears that he is talking about the town of Puna here.

19 A piece of eight denoted an old Spanish dollar, which at the time was valued at around four shillings and sixpence.

20 See James Poling, *The Man Who Saved Robinson Crusoe*.

21 The poleaxe is a weapon like a battle-axe or a hatchet with a short handle and a sharp point at the back of its head. It was chiefly used to cut away rigging of an enemy ship while attempting to board her as well as to board an enemy vessel when the hull was too high by driving the points of several axes into the ship's sides to form a scaling wall.

22 According to Rogers they had six ships in the fleet at this time, though he does not say if this includes the *Dutchess* and the *Duke*.

23 The Morell brothers were able to buy back the *Ascensión*.

24 See James Poling, *The Man Who Saved Robinson Crusoe*.

25 In 1696 an Italian, Gamelli Careri, took passage on one of these Spanish galleons and wrote about it. Rogers had the English translation in his cabin.

26 In other parts of this book we have said Rogers made a fortune from this voyage; some historians say he did. This figure comes from Bryan Little's book.

27 The *Mariner's Mirror*, 15 (1929), pp. 67–8.

28 This was recorded in the Committee of SPCK Minutes, 16 April 1716, Item 22.

29 See Daniel Defoe, *A General History of the Pyrates* (originally published in 1724; repr. and ed. Manuel Schonhorn, Dover Publications, 1973).

30 Taken from Defoe, *The Pyrates*, pp. 646–7.

31 Much of this account of the trial is also taken from Defoe, *The Pyrates*.

32 Captain Hildesley was in command of HMS *Flamborough* which had been stationed at Nassau during the crisis.

33 Rogers wanted to send Beauchamp to England since he was tired of the lack of response and help from the English government, but the time was not yet right for Beauchamp to go.

34 Bryan Little, *Crusoe's Captain*.

35 Much of the information in this chapter comes from Colonial Office papers volumes CO 13 and CO 23 and from Colonial State Papers, volumes 1716–1732.

36 The *Mariner's Mirror*, 15 (1929), pp. 67–8.

37 From the Journal of the Board of Trade and Plantations.

38 From Harcourt Malcolm, *A History of the Bahamas House of Assembly* (1921), ch. 6.
39 These were in fact no more than shacks: as we have seen, proper houses were not built until Rogers arrived.

Further Reading

A Cruising Voyage Round the World, Woodes Rogers (The Narrative Press, repr. 2004).

Crusoe's Captain, Bryan Little (Odhams Press, 1960).

The Funnel of Gold, Mendel Peterson (Little, Brown and Co., 1975).

A General History of the Pyrates, Daniel Defoe, ed. Manuel Schonhorn, (Dover Publications, 1973).

A History of the Bahamas House of Assembly, Malcolm Harcourt (1921).

History of the Pirates, Charles Johnson (Conway Maritime Press, 1998).

Life Aboard a British Privateer in the Time of Queen Anne, Being the Journal of Woodes Rogers, Robert C. Leslie (Chapman and Hall, 1894).

The Man Who Saved Robinson Crusoe, James Poling (World's Work, 1967).

Under the Black Flag, David Cordingly (Random House, 1995).

Index